Don't Tick Off the Gators!

Managing Problems Before Problems Manage You

An Irreverent Guide to Dealing with Problems and Crises in Your Professional and Personal Life

JIM GRIGSBY

Rainbow Books, Inc.
FLORIDA

Library of Congress Cataloging-in-Publication Data

Grigsby, Jim, 1953–
  Don't tick off the gators! : managing problems before problems manage you, an irreverent guide to dealing with problems and crises in your professional and personal life / Jim Grigsby.— 1st ed.
    p. cm.
  Includes bibliographical references and index.
  ISBN 1-56825-106-8 (pbk. : alk. paper)
  1. Problem solving. 2. Crisis management. 3. Adaptability (Psychology) 4. Resilience (Personality trait) 5. Success in business—Psychological aspects. I. Title: Managing problems before problems manage you. II. Title.
    HD30.29.G745 2005
    658.4'03—dc22
                              2005012349

Don't Tick Off the Gators! © 2006 by Jim Grigsby
ISBN-10: 1-56825-106-8
ISBN-13: 978-1-56825-106-6

Published by
Rainbow Books, Inc., P. O. Box 430, Highland City, FL 33846-0430

Editorial Offices and Wholesale/Distributor Orders
Telephone: (863) 648-4420 • Email: RBIbooks@aol.com

Individuals' Orders
Toll-free Telephone (800) 431-1579 • www.AllBookStores.com

All rights reserved. No part of this book may be reproduced or transmitted in any form or by any means, electronic or mechanical (except as follows for photocopying for review purposes). Permission for photocopying can be obtained for internal or personal use, the internal or personal use of specific clients, and for educational use, by paying the appropriate fee to

Copyright Clearance Center, 222 Rosewood Dr.
Danvers, MA 01923 U.S.A.

The names, characters, locations and events depicted in this book are fictitious and products of the author's imagination and are not based on actual events. Any resemblances to actual events, locations, companies, or persons, living or dead, is entirely coincidental.

∞ The paper used in this publication meets the minimum requirements of the American National Standard for Information Sciences—Permanence of Paper for Printed Library Materials, ANSI Z39.48-1984.

First Edition 2006
12 11 10 09 08 07 06   7 6 5 4 3 2 1
Printed in the United States of America

For Tina, with love and thanks.

Contents

Acknowledgments   ix

Introduction   11
    One — *Remember the Original Mission*   13
    Two — *Is the Original Mission Still Valid?*   21
    Three — *Focus on the Hungriest Gator*   25
    Four — *Find the Safest Way Out*   33
    Five — *Little Help?*   39
    Six — *Don't Aggravate the Gators*   43
    Seven — *Shovel My Way Out or Dig Deeper?*   47
    Eight — *Find the Gators Another Source of Food*   53
    Nine — *Change the Mission and Save Limbs*   57
    Ten — *What Would McGyver Do?*   61
    Eleven — *If You Have Weapons, Use Them Wisely*   65

CONTENTS

Twelve — *Are the Gators More Afraid than You?*   71

Thirteen — *How Did This Happen?*
               Can I Prevent It in the Future?   77

Fourteen — *Stop Shaking—It Doesn't Help*   83

Fifteen — *Act Brave, You Might Fool the Gators*   89

Sixteen — *Complete Your Plan*   97

Seventeen — *Is the Plan Flexible?*   107

Eighteen — *Make the Plan Work*   113

Nineteen — *Get Out of the Swamp*   119

Twenty — *Relax, You've Earned It*   125

Twenty-One — *Solve the Problems*   131

Twenty-Two — *Start Again, a Bit Wiser*   139

Twenty-Three — *Don't Taunt the Gators*   147

Twenty-Four — *The Lessons*   155

Suggested Reading   159

Index   161

About the Author   167

Acknowledgments

Thanks to Tina for her love, faith, and guidance. Without her, this book would not have been completed.

Thanks to Johnny Holland for having the day that inspired the concept.

Thanks to my parents, Marj and Bert Grigsby, for teaching me about responsibility and persistence.

Thanks to The Godson, Alec Holland, for being my favorite gator.

Thanks to Betty Wright and Betsy Wright-Lampe of Rainbow Books for believing in the value of my book and guiding me through the process.

Thanks to all the people who helped me—you know who you are!

Thanks to God for the talent to write this book and for making these wonderful people part of my life.

Introduction

Every day you encounter problems at work and at home. Problems arrive, hang around long enough to annoy, then leave; soon new and different ones replace them. Problems and crises are like alligators: menacing, slippery, and frightening. You fear they will consume you in one quick bite.

Some problems sneak up on you like gators in the water. You see a pair of big, dark eyes, barely above the water line, staring at you as the gator inches closer. The eyeballs, just above the surface, are analogous to some problems—problems that are deeper than they first appear or that hide the true danger. These are your personal gators.

Unfortunately, some people give the gators control of their lives. They react to small inconveniences just as forcefully as to major problems. They equate a wet newspaper to a transmission repair bill.

For others, the effect is cumulative. Problems pile up for days or weeks until they react to every event as if it were an organized attack by a SWAT Team.

When the alligators surround you, how you react sets the stage for your ability to solve the problem. In difficult situations, your initial reaction can compound the problem and inadvertently tick off the gators, setting you up for an unfavorable outcome.

Failure to accurately assess the situation can also impact the solution. Without an accurate assessment, how can you formulate a plan that will solve the problem?

Your wife gives you bad news, and you yell at her. Your husband asks why you need to buy a new picnic set, and you explode. Your boss decides he wants more changes to the proposal, and you lash out at your staff—the people you need to help complete the proposal.

To better handle stress, you need to remember the First Law of the Swamp:

Don't Tick Off The Gators!

If the gators are angry or hungry, they will not react kindly to you flogging or kicking them. Keep your cool and focus on solving the problems. Set the anger aside for later. Analyze the situation, review your options, and formulate a rational plan to solve the problem.

Okay, if you aren't always capable of separating your feelings from the situation, what can you do?

I'm not a psychologist, but I have been surrounded by alligators many times and have learned a few lessons. Some of these lessons will provide guidance for you to use when the gators surround you.

One day, during a phone call, my best friend Johnny Holland said, "Man, I'm having one of those days, up to my ass in alligators."

My advice to him was, "Don't tick off the gators."

By applying the lessons illustrated in the following chapters, it is possible to escape the gators in your life. But don't expect a totally serious book; at times like this you need humor.

ONE

Remember the Original Mission

Have you ever seen the poster depicting a soldier, shovel in hand, standing in a swamp, surrounded by alligators? Below the picture is the caption, "When you're up to your behind in alligators, it is difficult to remember the original mission was to drain the swamp!"

It's true. Whether your crisis is major or minor, it helps to remember why you are there and what you intend to do. To get out of the swamp you need to overcome the urge to react and take control of the situation. You need to ask:

Why am I here, and what was I supposed to do?

Once you focus on the mission, you begin to understand how you became a potential lunch for the gators. If the mission is to drain the swamp and you forget to bring the pumps and hoses, you learn a valuable lesson: double-check the equipment *before* the mission.

If you focus on your goal and know what you want to accomplish, it is easier to place the current problem in perspective. The soldier on the poster has an urgent problem—preserving his life and limbs; that is more important than draining the swamp. Is your crisis life-threatening, or is it less perilous?

Knowing the depth of your problem and how it relates to your mission is vital.

> Nick Koufax read the note taped to his office door and felt a twinge in his chest. "Bring your coffee to my office. Thanks, Jay."
>
> *The boss wants to see me first thing Monday morning?*
>
> Grabbing a large University of Michigan mug and his portfolio, he walked to the coffee station. After filling the mug, he trudged toward Jay Young's office. While walking, he tried to determine why he was being summoned so early on a Monday morning. He was baffled. He could not remember any mistakes or forgotten work. Straining his memory for anything remotely connected to an error, he still came up with nothing. He couldn't think of anything that warranted a trip to the woodshed.
>
> As a project analyst for Champion Technology Solutions, he was usually praised for his reports. His boss, Jay Young, and a satisfied client both lauded his last analysis report as superior.
>
> Mystified about the reason for the meeting, Nick turned the corner and walked into Jay's office. Tentatively, he greeted the boss, "Good morning, Jay. What's up?"
>
> Peering over his half-moon glasses, Jay Young smiled warmly. "Nick, glad to see you. How was the weekend?"
>
> Feeling even more wary, Nick replied, "Fine, I got in a couple rounds on Lakeside. Yours?"
>
> "Very relaxing." Realizing his employee's anxiety, Jay spoke apologetically, "Sorry about the note. I've been here since seven, and it feels like noon to me. Around eight, I received a call from Waner Industries that might interest you."
>
> Settling into a chair, Nick stared at his boss, waiting for him to continue.
>
> "They've asked me to attend their board meeting this Friday morning to update them on the status of our computer

installation. Management decided they want us to provide monthly reports. They want us to keep them informed about the progress of their investment. Remember how reluctant they were to approve the expenditure for the project?"

Nick nodded as he sipped coffee.

"That is where you come in. You're my best analyst; I know I can count on you. Your work is concise and thorough. I need you to create a presentation for me in PowerPoint. This is top priority, so put everything else aside and deliver me a winner."

Nick beamed, "Thanks, I will." Exhilaration quickly replaced tension.

"This report needs the diamond touch. I want it looking like we paid for it—charts, graphs, indexed, and bound. It is important to me that they are impressed with Champion. I need something that impresses them visually, verbally, and on paper. Am I clear?"

"Yes, sir. How soon do you want to see the first draft?"

Jay removed his glasses, leaned forward on his elbows, and spoke in a measured tone, "That is the challenging part. We, actually you, do not have the luxury of time. The board meeting is Friday morning, but I need to leave here Wednesday afternoon. I'm driving down to the capital for a seminar and won't return until late Thursday night. I need it by three Wednesday afternoon."

Nick whistled. *Great, he doesn't just want a report, but one that makes him look good to the board. And by Wednesday afternoon. No problem.*

"Jay, I'll get started right away. What points do you want to emphasize?" Rising from his chair, he thought he felt an alligator tail hit him in the shins.

"They need to see that the project is progressing as we planned and that they are getting more value than expected." He thought for a moment. "I know you can do it."

Nick walked out, proud that Jay was so confident in him. He also knew this was one project he could not screw up.

Working all day Monday and late into the evening Tuesday,

Nick pored over financial reports, progress reports, change orders, client update memos, and internal e-mails.

The status reports indicated that the hardware and network configurations were complete, the network cables were installed, and the software development was on schedule. Training was behind schedule, but that did not concern him. They could schedule a make up class next week.

Nick's frustration level rose when he tried to estimate the bottom-line impact of the project. He created several expense-versus-cost projections, comparing them with the expected income; yet, he couldn't prove that Waner was getting more bang for their buck.

Part of his frustration was directed at the project manager, who was not up to date on her billing, specifically the invoices for change orders. That alone prevented him from knowing if the project was within the budget. In his mind, he heard one question echoing, "Will it finish under budget or not?"

Nick was tired, frustrated, and battling the I'm-never-going-to-get-this-right blues. His mind drifted to his most recent meeting with Jay. He was deeply engrossed in thought and did not notice two very old gators enter his office.

Earlier that day after lunch at his desk he had presented Jay a draft for review. Jay, in the midst of a short workweek, as well, and trying to accomplish as much, if not more work than Nick, gave it a high-level read and asked, "Where's the financial information?"

Nick's promise to include it in the next draft tomorrow morning was acknowledged with a curt, "Fine."

Jay returned to the present, lowered his head, and worked late into the evening. He and the janitor walked out together after ten o'clock.

Arriving at the office before seven Wednesday morning, Nick doubted he could complete the assignment on time. It bothered him that he still didn't know if the project would finish under budget or not. Handing an incomplete report to Jay Young was not an option or a wise career move.

His doubt turned to panic when he recalled some of Jay

> Young's legendary reactions to failure. Closed doors didn't obstruct the sound, so everyone in the area heard the yelling and one-sided conversation. He had witnessed several men and women as they walked out of Jay's office, visibly shaken.
> Nick knew Jay was insufferable when disappointed. In his inimitable style Jay would let everyone in the department, probably the entire company, know exactly what and how Nick screwed up. He felt doomed.
> The pair of old but vibrant alligators began inching closer to Nick as the deadline approached.

Nick forgets his mission and invests time worrying about what he cannot do, not what he needs to do. Instead of wasting time and allowing his frustration to build, he needs to accomplish something meaningful—finish the report.

The next time you are in a similar situation, remember that you can accomplish more by working toward the goal than you can by worrying. Your first priority is to review the situation. Stop, take a deep breath, and determine the real problem. Figure out how you ended up in a swamp surrounded by hungry alligators. Then ask yourself:

What was I supposed to do?

Shift your focus from worrying and fear of failure to the purpose of your mission. Remember the original mission—what it is that you are supposed to accomplish. Once you focus on the goal, you can start to solve the problems that prevent you from completing your mission. Isn't that what you really want to do?

> Nick Koufax needed a break. His mind felt full and cluttered, and he was thirsty. He walked down a flight of stairs to the employee lounge to grab a bottle of orange juice.
> Two alligators kept pace with him from a safe distance.
> Staring at him from one of the tables was the front page of a tabloid, with predictions for the coming year. He grunted and said to himself, "Like they can predict the future any better than I can predict the financial outcome of

the Waner Project. What a waste of time. Why don't they print something more important like the latest sighting of Big Foot?"

His own words hit him like a slap to the side of the head. He was wasting *his* time trying to predict the future of the project. Nick realized he was caught up making financial projections, instead of analyzing the reported expenditures and billed income. It was then that he remembered his mission—report the status of the project. Jay Young and the Waner board could worry about the future.

Nick finished his drink and returned to his desk with renewed focus and a sense of purpose. In less than an hour, he completed the presentation. He supplemented the status report with graphs, charts, and financial reports. The charts depicted reported and billed costs versus budgeted costs, while the graphs compared the financial performance to the project plan.

Enlivened by adrenalin and ignoring frayed nerves, Nick burst into Jay's office and handed him a diskette containing the completed work. As Jay examined each slide in detail before moving on to the next one, Nick paced and watched apprehensively.

After what seemed like hours, Jay finished his review and turned toward Nick. He grinned: "This is great work. I knew you would come through. Thank you."

"Thanks, I'll copy the diskette, take it to the Media department, and have the reports bound while I'm at lunch." Relief was evident in every syllable. "Jay, I do have one question, though, one that is driving me insane."

"What's that?"

"How will you explain the financial projections to Waner's board?"

Jay studied the ceiling before answering, "I don't intend to. My job is to present the facts. Theirs is to interpret them. I think the work you did will lead reasonable people to believe the project will finish close to budget. That's all anyone can ask at this point. Unless they can predict the future."

"Right."

Two disappointed alligators slowly left the building. On the way out, they remembered an article in the tabloid about the newly discovered health benefits of gator meat. They decided to visit the publishers to discuss a difference of opinion on that subject.

Nick's mission is to provide information for Jay Young's report to the board, not to predict the outcome of the project. He is sidetracked for a while when he loses focus and concentrates on the wrong items. When he refocuses and concentrates on what he is supposed to do—his original mission—he is able to complete the report.

Overcomplicating the mission is an invitation for alligators to swim toward you, anticipating a meal. And you are the meal they have in mind.

TWO

Is the Original Mission Still Valid?

Have circumstances changed since the mission began? If so, you need to recognize that and change your plan to fit the new situation. It doesn't make sense to continue digging a hole if it fills up with water each time you strike bottom. Why walk directly into the jaws of gators when you can avoid them?

> Drake Banks didn't know how to tell his boss he wouldn't meet the deadline for his assignment. Last Friday, Leslie McGraw gave him one week to compile a training manual for the company's newest client. The deadline was tomorrow.
> As member of the education and training department for Diamond Medical Billing Services, Drake did both grunt work and classroom training, and the manual was definitely grunt work. Grunt work or not, he had too much pride to try and coast through the assignment.
> Writing training manuals for medical office billers was tedious. Health care billing could be very complex and required a lot of step-by-step instructions. No manual was complete

> unless it contained every pertinent computer screen shot as a visual aid to the students.
>
> Leslie McGraw made it clear that she wanted the work completed on time so she could review the manual over the weekend. After she gave Drake her changes, he would prepare the final version for delivery to the printer the next day.
>
> Staring at the stack of papers that would become the manual, Drake knew he had completed about eighty percent of the job. Unfortunately, the remaining twenty percent was more work than he could complete in one day, let alone one afternoon.
>
> The unfinished sections were the chapters about secondary billing (billing a patient's second insurance after the primary or first insurance pays on the bill). They contained complex information about a number of payment scenarios. Each scenario required a separate group of computer screen prints. Drake knew it would take two days to complete the project and was not comfortable asking Leslie for additional time.
>
> Three alligators moved into Drake's cubicle, situating themselves near the exit. They sensed dead meat every time he moaned.

Drake has a common problem. He knows what needs to be done but doesn't know how to do it without appearing incompetent. He needs to ask for more time, but is afraid that if he does, Leslie will consider him a failure.

Many people are afraid to approach their boss with a problem. They imagine the worst possible reaction, and their minds work overtime amplifying it. Fear grips their minds.

One way to alleviate that fear is to present a solution to the problem, not just the problem. Presenting a solution demonstrates clear thought and analytical ability. Drake will soon realize this.

> Drake was multi-tasking: printing screen shots, collating the chapters, labeling dividers, and worrying about how to tell Leslie that he could not meet the deadline. Unable to eliminate the fear and concentrate on his work, he decided to do something to occupy his mind. He read his backlog of email.

He read one email twice to make sure he wasn't seeing things. He wasn't and had been handed a gift. Earlier in the day, the project manager had sent an email indicating a change in the training schedule.

The new client, a large multi-physician clinic, requested a one-week delay in training. Because school physicals continued into the week scheduled for training, they were unable to send employees to training while handling their patient load.

Drake rolled his neck and felt the tightness recede. His shoulders also loosened when he thought of the extra time he had been given to complete the manual. Or so he hoped. "The client's needs have changed, so I shouldn't have to meet the same internal deadline. It wouldn't make sense, would it?" he wondered.

He cleared his mind, put the work aside, and thought about how to convince Leslie he needed more time.

As he centered his thoughts on the mission and changed requirements, an idea formed. He thought, I need to approach her in a positive fashion, offering a solution. I'll show her what I've accomplished and explain how we can deliver a quality training manual for the client with a little more time.

Tapping on the keyboard, he wrote and rewrote a memo until he was satisfied it conveyed his thoughts and plan.

A while later, seated in Leslie's office, Drake inhaled sharply, "Mrs. McGraw, I mean, Leslie, I need to discuss the clinic training manual with you. In light of the new schedule, I think we can give them an even better manual if I can have two more days to complete it."

"Really? Tell me what you have in mind."

Her positive reply put Drake at ease. This is going to work, he thought.

Handing her the memo, he launched into a rapid explanation about the complexities of secondary billing. He also mentioned the importance of accurate screenshots and instructions in a training manual. "Tomorrow afternoon I will give you what I have completed. I will deliver the final two sections to you Tuesday, well ahead of the new training schedule."

> Leslie McGraw smiled, "Drake, you can exhale now. I think that is an excellent idea. Good work."
> Walking back to his cubicle Drake Banks smiled at the thought of her parting words, "I'm very impressed with your ability to think in a crisis. That kind of thinking is what I look for in a supervisor."
> Three disappointed gators exited his cubicle in search of less resilient prey.

Drake Banks's promise to complete the assignment, based on changed circumstances, attests to his ability to see beyond a problem and propose a solution. His boss commends him for recognizing the change, for honestly analyzing his capacity to deliver a quality document, and for offering a viable solution.

Remember the original mission and determine if the circumstances warrant a change in your plan.

Three

Focus on the Hungriest Gator

Size does not matter. Hunger, however, does.
If one of the gators appears hungrier than the rest, he or she deserves your immediate attention. Do not attack an old, feeble alligator that shows no interest in you while you ignore the energetic one climbing over the others, intent on devouring you. A gator that is flashing teeth, and has its gaze fixed on you, is the one you need to worry about first.

> After a strenuous week in the securities business, Ben Seaver arrived home on a Friday evening, ready for a quiet evening and relaxing weekend. That changed when he was greeted by Dominick, his son, who reminded Ben that his school project was due Monday.
> "Dad, can you help me finish it, please?"
> Dominick and each member of his class had been asked to build a model, planned city: houses, businesses, streets, schools, parks, municipal services, and a mass transportation system. It must also include lawns, trees, and landscaping. To

further complicate the matter, his son's best friend, Dale Matthews, had already completed his, and it was fantastic.

"You should see it, Dad. Overhead monorails, alabaster buildings, an airport, traffic lights, and a baseball stadium with lights!"

Gators crawled into Ben Seaver's living room, eyeing his legs, confident of a rather delicious feast.

Ben sat on the edge of his recliner, removed his shoes, and studied the eager face in front of him. "Yes, son, I'll help you. Let me change my clothes, and we'll get started."

"Great. Thanks, Dad! I'll get the stuff set up in the garage."

Dominick dashed off, leaving Ben alone. Rubbing the back of his neck, Ben stared at nothing in particular and sighed, thinking, "I hope this project is easier than my week."

Walking into the garage, he asked, "Okay, sport, what do we need to do?"

"Dad, remember how we worked on this right after Easter?"

"Right. Let's see what we've already done, figure out what needs to be done, and then make a plan."

Father and son examined the work they started several weeks ago. Ben was sure that it was in the same state as when they last worked on it. "I remember us finishing the foundation board. What else did we do?"

Dominick stared at his dad. "The streets are done, yellow lines and all. We marked the building sites, too."

"What have you done since then?"

"Not much." Hands in pockets and head down, he mumbled, "Sorry. I guess I forgot about it."

Ben shook his head, then smiled, "That's okay. I did the same thing at your age. We'll both have to work on this all weekend, together. No goofing off for either of us. Understood?"

"Yes, sir."

"Find the green material your mom used for the place mats. Then bring it and the buildings from your train set. We need to take an inventory of what we have, figure out what we need to

do, and determine how much time it will take to do it."
Dominick nodded and ran into the house, eager to get started.

Dale Matthews and his dad Jude, an electrical engineer, build a futuristic geo-city that will overwhelm the class. Ben knows he can't compete with that; he doesn't possess that talent or time to build such a city. But competing with Jude Matthews is not the primary issue. Ben knows he and his son need to focus on completing the project on time, not on outdoing someone else's project.

He also wants to teach Dominick to take pride in his work—to do his best. Ben knows the project should reflect the work of a ten-year-old boy, with help from his father. It should not be the work of a thirty-five-year-old electrical engineer, with help from his son. Ben is concentrating on the hungriest gator—the project.

Dominick and his dad conducted an inventory of buildings, vehicles, people, and the train set (it will serve as the mass transit rail system). For a few minutes, they stood silently and stared at their diverse collection.

They soon realized they didn't have the elements to build a truly model city. The buildings were of dissimilar architectural designs, the vehicles were from two or three different decades, and the train was a late 1960s model. The people who would populate the town included Native Americans in war paint, baseball action figures, football players, soldiers in combat fatigues, and astronauts.

"Son, this will be an eclectic city—very diverse in design and in people. It may not compete with the fancier projects, but it will be the best we can do."

"I think it is very important for you to understand what I mean by the best we can do. We will combine our talents and resources, but this is your project. I'm here to help you. I'll help you create the best city you can. Do you understand what I mean?"

"Yes, sir." Dominick nodded, "Where do we begin?"

"It looks like we need to paint the buildings and touch up some of the foundation. Maybe add a lake in the park and a river along Main Street. What do you think?"

> "Okay. The park needs a baseball field and a soccer field. Oh, and a bike path, too."
>
> "Good thinking, son."

That evening Dominick and his dad stand side-by-side painting far past the youngster's normal bedtime. They both have other things they would have preferred to do, but right now neither seems to mind. Some accidental painting of each other's arms and hands enhances their time together.

After cleaning the paintbrushes, taking showers, and consuming two large bowls of popcorn, they are ready to turn in.

> "Son, you did a great job tonight."
> "Thanks, Dad. You, too."
> "Get some sleep; tomorrow is another day of work."
> "Good night."

The gators began to get bored and one or two waddled back to the swamp.

The next morning, over a breakfast of doughnuts and milk, father and son agreed that the cars and trucks they have just wouldn't look right in their beautiful city. Properly fueled, they journeyed downtown to purchase new vehicles.

On the way home Dominick asked, "When can we place the buildings on the foundation?"

"Once we make sure the paint is dry."

Using a finger to test the paint, Dominick pronounced it ready and began to construct his city. After several modifications, he looked at his dad and asked, "Well?"

> "Son, I think if you move the bridge closer to the center of the river, you'll have a winner. While you do that, I'll heat the glue gun and we can make the arrangement permanent. Good job!"

Ben Seaver creates an environment for success by identifying the objective—complete the project. At the same time, he eliminates an unneeded foe—trying to compete with an electrical engineer and failing. He and Dominick are on their way to completing the project on time.

Ben takes advantage of their time together to reinforce the importance of character. His words and his actions teach his young son about honesty, responsibility, and integrity.

Character is molded in many ways. Working against the clock is a good opportunity to demonstrate the value of character.

> Dominick outlined a route for the rapid transit system. It required them to relocate two buildings, but the effect was outstanding.
>
> Most components of the train set were in excellent condition; however, the tunnel needed a coat of paint and the water tower lacked one supporting strut. Dominick spent twenty minutes painting the tunnel, while Ben attempted to repair the water tower support.
>
> "This isn't going to work," Ben announced. "We'll have to get a new one."
>
> Dominick was a bit frustrated, because he thought they were almost through.
>
> "Son, we need to keep working. No pouting. The town needs a water system and it is your responsibility to see that they have one."
>
> "Yes, sir."
>
> "Anyone can work when things are going well. It takes a grown up person, even a 'young grown up', to keep working when he doesn't want to or when things get tough. The difference between a boy and a young man is that the young man will keep working, while the boy will quit."
>
> Dominick nodded and went back to work, intent on impressing his dad by not complaining.

All problems are not created equal—some are subsets of others. Solve the primary ones before attempting to defeat their progeny.

> Father and son enjoyed lunch at the local sub shop, then visited the hobby shop in search of new supports for the water tower. The water tower support was not available, but the store owner suggested they remove the other three truncheons

and substitute number-two pencils for the supports. "Paint them grey to match the reservoir and you will have a water tower as good as new."

"Thanks," came from both, nearly in unison.

At home they began to assemble the village, placing the green felt on the board to simulate lawns and parks. Next, Dominick determined final positions for the vehicles, water tower, and human figures.

Just before dinner, a tired voice piped up, "Dad, can we finish tomorrow? I'm bushed!"

Stepping back to examine their work, Ben smiled, "We're finished building it, buddy. What we need to do tomorrow is figure out how to place it in the van so it won't break when we drive it to school on Monday.

"You did a great job."

"Thanks, I couldn't have done it without you."

"Let's clean up and enjoy the evening."

Sunday, afternoon Dominick carefully placed the unattached items in storage crates, while Ben cleaned out the back of the van. "Seaverville" would fit securely on the floor for the trip to school.

Ben and Dominick avert a crisis by working together and focusing on the major issues, not the sidebars.

The remaining gators leave quietly and quickly. They are disappointed and vow to take it out on their next victim.

Deal with reality. Working through a crisis demands both physical and mental energy. Don't waste either by fighting make-believe foes. You have enough problems with hungry alligators without introducing imaginary foes.

Too many people get caught up in a self-defeating mind game. They imagine the worst possible result, such as being fired or publicly humiliated, no matter what they do. Or they beat themselves senseless for perceived shortcomings. Wasting time and energy neither solves nor simplifies a problem.

Focus on the major problems and solve them. Invest your time and energy wisely.

Alligators are attracted to the smell of fear, wasted time, wasted energy, and self-pity. Why work up a lather just to attract more gators?

If Ben Seaver spends his time trying to outshine Jude Matthews by building an elaborate metropolitan complex, it will be an exercise in frustration. He doesn't have the electrical engineer's talent or resources. If he spends the time berating himself because he doesn't have that talent, he will not focus on the important issue—completing the project on time.

Ben and Dominick will not finish a more complex version of the city by Monday morning. Creating a complex city will not be an enjoyable father-son project. More importantly, Ben will waste a prime opportunity to teach his son about integrity and the importance of completing his own work.

Don't attempt to solve all the problems at once. Instead, make an impact by solving the major ones, while keeping an eye on the smaller ones. The problems to solve first are the ones that can consume you first.

Focus on the hungriest gator.

FOUR

Find the Safest Way Out

How can you get temporary relief from your crisis and find a safe place to plan a successful, long-range strategy?

First, look for a clear path, preferably one free of gators, leading to a safer place. Sometimes the best route is not the closest or most visible; remember the admonishment of airline flight attendants, "The nearest exit may be behind you."

> Gunther Drysdale arrived at his office early each Monday morning to prepare for the operations meeting. As product development manager for a manufacturing firm, he briefed the management team about a number of active projects.
>
> Before he could fill his coffee mug, the phone rang. It was his boss, Reese MacPhail.
>
> "Gunther, can you come to my office right away? I've got someone here to see you."
>
> "Yes, sir. I'll be there in a minute."
>
> Gunther climbed a flight of stairs, wondering who would need to see him at seven o'clock on a Monday morning.

As he entered the CEO's outer office, he heard Reese speaking with a woman. Her voice was familiar, but he couldn't identify her.

"Gunther, good to see you." Reese turned toward the young woman seated on his sofa and continued without waiting for a reply, "You remember Matilda Caldwell, your summer intern? She's ready to start a week early. Isn't that great? Eager and ready to learn!"

Gunther tried to hide his surprise, "Good morning, Reese."

Speaking almost automatically, he extended a hand to the rising young lady. "Matilda, good to see you again. I didn't expect you until next week."

"Mr. Drysdale, I decided to skip the family vacation and get right to work. I hope that isn't inconvenient for you."

Reese roared, "Nonsense! Gunther is just as anxious to have you start as you are to get started. Isn't that right?"

Gunther forced himself to speak slowly and calmly, "Yes, sir. We can always use the help."

"Wonderful. She and my niece, Amanda, arrived Saturday and told me they were ready to start today. Amanda is going to work in accounting."

Gunther sensed a set up, but managed to smile.

"Why don't you give Matilda another tour of the operations and then get her started on all that blasted paperwork for human resources."

Looking at Matilda, Gunther softened a bit, "Matilda, welcome aboard. I think we can keep you busy and challenged this summer. Let's get started."

He and Matilda retraced the steps he took just a few minutes before. Neither observed four small and aggressive alligators following them.

Gunther's week is off to a great start—ambushed by his boss before his first cup of coffee. Gunther also thinks that Reese knew about the change in start dates weeks ago, but conveniently forgot to tell him.

He ends the internal pity party and remembers how impressed he was with Matilda during the interviews. He also wants to make her feel welcome, knowing that a bright and eager person around will lighten the workload for his staff.

If you find yourself in a situation where your game plan is changed by someone else, what can you do? For some the first impulse is to scream or throw a tantrum. Fortunately for the rest of us, society frowns on primal behavior. We need to respond with a bit more control.

To escape your personal, alligator-filled swamp, you need to remain calm. Chill out. Take a deep breath to clear your mind, as well as your lungs. Your exit strategy will not miraculously materialize while you are yelling or exhibiting childish behavior. You need a clear and calm mind to develop a plan.

> "How do I manage to pull this one off?" echoed in Gunther's mind. "I had no idea what I was going to have her work on next week, let alone today. Think, buddy boy, think."
>
> Gunther gave Matilda a condensed tour and briefly described the functions performed in each area. He spoke from memory, while part of his brain tried to come up with something for her to do the rest of the day. After introducing her to the people in his department, the tour ended at an empty desk, ten feet from his office door.
>
> "Don't try to remember everyone's name and everything we do here. We'll schedule time for you to observe and learn how each section fits into the big picture. Think of this department as a jigsaw puzzle. The pieces will eventually fit into place."
>
> "Thanks, I'll try to do that. I want to be an asset, not a detriment."
>
> "You will definitely add value to the department, sooner than you think. For now, why don't you check out the desk and see what supplies you need. I'll be back shortly."
>
> Walking away from Matilda, he remembered the operations meeting and his unfinished report—the one he came in early to complete. Fortunately, the meeting was to start at ten, over an hour away.
>
> Gunther walked toward Deborah Andrews, the department's administrative assistant. Quietly, he explained

the situation and asked if she could teach Matilda the intricacies of the telephone system and help her complete a requisition form for office supplies.

"Not a problem, we can keep her busy for hours with paperwork and the phone system."

"Thanks. I hate to dump this on you, but I need to get ready for the Operations meeting."

Deborah smiled. "Leave her to me. She can start the company tutorial. By the time you return she will be an expert on our voice mail and the company Intranet."

"Great. I hadn't thought of that."

Rolling his neck to untie a knot of muscles, he stepped into his office and dove into his report.

The gators talked among themselves, hoping he would relax. They don't like to chew on tough meat; they preferred relaxed victims because they were much easier to digest.

Working quickly, but thoroughly, Gunther updated last week's department report and printed several copies. Studying the agenda for today's meeting and jotting down a few questions, he placed a legal pad inside his meeting binder and took a last gulp of coffee.

As he passed Deborah's desk, he smiled and whispered, "Thank you for your help."

"By the way, I just spoke with human resources. Someone will be here at eleven to help Matilda complete the paperwork. They didn't know she was starting today, either. Go figure."

Gunther rolled his eyes toward the ceiling and Reese's office.

"You need to lighten up, man. Life is full of surprises. Do you need to reschedule any appointments?"

"Yes, I do. On both counts."

"Got you covered. I'll spread them out over the next few days. Now, get going, Reese won't like it if you are late!"

"Right."

Gunther stopped at Matilda's desk, " Is everything going okay?"

Don't Tick Off the Gators!   37

"Yes. Mrs. Andrews is taking great care of me."
"Good. I'll meet with you after lunch to brief you on the current projects and give you your first assignment." *As soon as I figure that out myself.*
"Great. I can't wait to get started on something besides paperwork."
He smiled in agreement and walked away.
Lindsay Walters stopped Gunther to discuss a minor problem with a new product.
"Walk to the conference room with me. We can talk on the way."
Chatting as they walked to the conference room, he answered her questions, and then asked for a favor. "Can you ask Matilda to join you at lunch so she won't have to eat alone on her first day?"
"Sure, boss."
"Thanks, I appreciate that. Ask Deborah for two lunch vouchers."
Four disappointed gators skulk away in single file, looking for a new victim.

Gunther's morning isn't a total disaster because he identifies the real problem: managing his time against the unanticipated demands placed upon it. He avoids disaster and the gators by recognizing his priorities. He needs to attend the operations meeting and provide orientation for Matilda. Everything else can wait.

Clear thinking and a willingness to delegate allow him to accomplish both objectives. He makes Matilda feel welcome and prepared for the meeting, achieving both objectives in a very professional manner.

Gunther Drysdale solves his problems with a solution that is more than just an escape. He stops fretting and analyzes the situation, then determines what he can do. By focusing on the positive—the *I can* and not the negative—the *I can't*, Gunther solves his problem. Once he finds the safest way out, he uses it to accomplish his objectives. The ability to see beyond problems and develop solutions is the measure of professional manager.

Gunther, with help from Deborah Andrews, develops and implements a plan to complete his mission. Even though someone else changes his mission, he finds a path to a safe place and gets rid of the gators.

FIVE

Little Help?

Why struggle alone if there are people who can help you fend off the gators?

A crisis is no time for macho posturing or a "John Wayne" mentality. If help is available, ask for it and use it. When you are in a swamp, help can come from people on dry land or from boats speeding to your rescue.

The sudden arrival of a speedboat that scares the gators and can transport you to dry land should be welcomed. Don't think that accepting help is a sign of weakness. You want to defeat the gators, either alone or with help.

Let's examine the actions of a harried young professional. How will he react when faced with a work overload? Will he ask for and accept assistance or will he try to do everything himself?

Archibald Kiner faced a deadline: he had to complete a department status report by close of business tomorrow. It was almost lunchtime and he was still writing the first draft. Actually, he stopped writing twenty minutes ago and began fretting about the consequence of not completing the report—unemployment.

Two days ago he requested the year-to-date budget variance spreadsheets from the finance department, but they had not arrived. Without them, he couldn't proceed.

He was behind on another report, as well, the weekly cash projection report, that was due tomorrow. His sense of dread was compounded when he remembered he had not revised the audit policy, an assignment he'd ignored for weeks.

Checking his PDA, he saw that his daughter had a soccer game in the afternoon that he'd promised to attend. Panic gripped him and tossed him head-first into a swamp populated by underfed gators.

Mrs. Hudson, the grandmotherly department administrative assistant, sensed his frustration and asked how she could help.

Hesitantly, he told her that he had asked Melvin Cavendish for the variance spreadsheets two days ago. "I don't think Cavendish understands my urgency. I've called twice and visited him once. He blows me off with 'I'll get to them as soon as I can.'"

Knowing how much Archibald had to do, she smiled. "Let me make a call to the vice president of finance; he owes us a favor."

"Did you know that Katrina Evans is looking for something to do? Maybe she can complete the cash projections for you. Will that help?"

Archibald smiled and stammered, "You bet. Thanks! You are a lifesaver."

Returning his smile, Mrs. Hudson started walking back to her desk. She half-turned and noticed Archibald taking long, loping strides toward Katrina's office.

Archibald makes two classic errors, common to new managers. The first mistake is trying to complete three projects without help, especially when he can delegate one to a very capable person. Katrina is bright, ambitious, and constantly asking for more work. After today, he can assign the cash projection report to her. His second error is not asking for help. The second time Cavendish rebuffed him, he should have asked his boss or Mrs. Hudson for assistance. Mrs. Hudson's offer to call the vice president of finance is no accident. She knows *their* boss needs this project completed on time and she will help make that happen.

> Archibald returned from lunch and found the budget variance spreadsheets on his desk. After a thank-you call to Mrs. Hudson, he began adding that information into his report.
>
> Once he possessed the spreadsheets, Archibald concentrated on his report, completed it on time, and attended his daughter's game, as promised.
>
> The gators swam away from Archibald and toward Cavendish for a quick meal of dead meat.

Our hero completes the report the next morning, well before the deadline. In the process, Archibald Kiner learns the value of asking for and accepting help and is able to focus on his problems and escape from the gators. Then he treats Mrs. Hudson and Katrina Evans to lunch to express his gratitude for their help.

Ask for and accept help. It is a sign of applied intelligence, not weakness.

SIX

Don't Aggravate the Gators

Once you successfully escape the eminent threat of being eaten alive by gators, don't aggravate them further. As you exit the swamp, do not exacerbate the situation by doing or saying something stupid.

Keep your mouth closed. Don't lash out at an alligator just because you feel good about your escape. Gators are genetically engineered to attack and feast on the haughty.

Save the gloating for later and focus your energy on solutions, not silly antics. You still need to solve the same problems that led you into the swamp; they did not magically disappear just because you escaped.

> Alexandra Jenkins, district manager for Throneberry Investments, was assigned the unpleasant task of developing a plan to close two Midwest division offices. Warren Alston, the pompous regional vice president, wanted to "cut the deadwood" and eliminate offices with operating losses.
>
> The assignment was difficult professionally and stressful personally. Alexandra felt close to most of the staff because

she hired and trained many of the employees, including both managers. She fought with Warren for several weeks to save the offices, but he insisted that she close them or "look for another job."

Several large gators caught the red-eye from Florida to Chicago, rented a luxury SUV, and headed for Alexandra's office. They were sleepy, hungry, and ready to devour her.

On the dreaded day the report was due, she received a call from Elizabeth Montgomery, the COO. Ms. Montgomery wanted to personally inform her that "Mr. Alston is no longer with the company and *his* plan to close the offices is on hold until senior management makes a final decision."

Then she asked Alexandra if the offices could be saved.

"Yes, ma'am. With some additional training, focused marketing, and hard work, we can turn them around."

"Then I suggest you start that right away. I want a plan for saving them on my desk before the close of business tomorrow."

"Yes, ma'am. I started to prepare one for Mr. Alston. I can promise you it will be completed by then. Thank you."

Notice how Ms. Montgomery never allows Alexandra the opportunity to celebrate Alston's departure? Instead, she focuses Alexandra's efforts to solve the problem.

Alexandra might be elated that Warren Alston is gone but she has a more important task at hand: developing a plan to save her branches.

Two of the alligators catch colds and decide to head back to Florida.

Alexandra started by reading the plan she wanted to present to Alston weeks ago. She knew it might be her only opportunity to save the offices. After a few minutes, the answer began to gel in her mind and she rushed to get it on paper. Grabbing several training and advertising manuals, she all but sprinted into her conference room. Using the speakerphone, she organized a conference call with her branch managers.

"Ladies and gentlemen, we need to spend whatever time it takes today developing a plan to save the offices in Fort Wayne and Kalamazoo."

An avid reader, Alexandra had read *Don't Tick Off the Gators* from cover to cover. She knew the project to save the two offices required more than just her ideas, and she valued the input of her managers. Her time and energy remained focused on her mission—saving the branch offices. She also resisted the temptation to waste energy gloating over Alston's demise.

The remaining gators called their travel agent and re-booked their flight back to Miami. On their way out of the office, they spotted an envelope with Warren Alston's home address. One asks the others, "Have you ever been to Naperville?"

Simplify, don't complicate.

Your objective is to solve the problem, not compound it. Once you escape from danger, don't slip back into a swamp filled with eager reptiles.

Alexandra and her managers invested nearly three hours in a brainstorming session. The result was several aggressive marketing strategies for the Kalamazoo and Fort Wayne branch managers to implement. They also agreed to develop a condensed training program by the end of the week.

The managers and Alexandra decided to schedule bi-monthly calls to improve communication between the branches and to make sure everyone was familiar with the company's investment strategies.

Alexandra Jenkins proved that she was an excellent manager by staying focused, solving the problem with help from her managers, and by saving two branch offices from closing.

The gators found their way to Naperville and enjoyed a fabulous meal of roasted Alston.

SEVEN

Shovel My Way Out or Dig Deeper?

Your goal remains the same: to complete the mission and solve the problem(s) that place you in the gator-filled swamp. You do not want to complicate the problems through your own actions or words. Instead, you want to focus your time and efforts on solving the crisis without creating bigger problems.

You have not solved the problem; you have *temporarily* escaped the gators. Remember that hungry alligators have been known to climb out of the water and pursue their prey on dry land. Do you want them to join you on what you thought was safe ground?

Use the shovel wisely. Dig your way out; do not dig in deeper.

Everyone isn't as wise as Alexandra Jenkins was in the previous chapter. Submitted for your approval is Chad Allen.

> Around three o'clock, the office manager, Mr. Sutton, summoned Chad Allen and Benton Williams into his office. His message was succinct; their proposal for Skinner Construction was "not acceptable."
>
> "You describe our products, but do not tell Skinner the

benefits to him. He needs to know how we can help him, not what we do. You need to revise this report today."

Looking from one man to another, he continued explaining, "Guys, this is a big account for an important and influential client. It needs to be the best work we can turn out. No excuses and no exceptions."

He turned to Chad and their eyes locked. "As an experienced project manager, I expect better work than this from you, Chad. Now, get it done."

Before either man could reply, the telephone rang. As Sutton answered it, he waved the two employees out of his office.

As Chad and Benton walked out, Chad muttered angrily, "You jerk. You told us to describe the products, and we did. *Now* you say we need to explain the benefits."

The two men entered Chad's office, not noticing several alligators congregating in the far corner, patiently waiting for a banquet of two.

Chad continued his tirade to Benton, harping on Sutton's inconsistency. Then a brilliant idea came into his mind. Or so he thought. "I'll make him eat his own words."

The alligators heard that and smiled.

Benton's eyes widened and he looked at his co-worker quizzically. "What are you going to do?"

"Find the original job memo and stuff it down his fat neck. He said, 'Describe the products,' and we did. If he thinks he can tell me to do better work to cover his mistake, then he is dead wrong."

"I don't know. We just need to alter a few paragraphs, add the benefits, and insert an ROI table, like we did for Carruthers and Sons. That shouldn't take too long."

"Go ahead, buddy boy. I'm going golfing this evening. No sense in wasting a beautiful July evening working. Just as soon as I find that idiot's memo—"

Benton shook his head and walked back to his office wondering why Chad was so gung-ho about making a point. He thought, Even if he does find the memo, we still need to change the proposal.

As Chad rifled through the Skinner file, searching for the "smoking gun memo," the gators set up a video camera to capture Chad's self-basting. They phoned in an order for table linen, china, and cutlery from Saks. This was a dream come true—a man actually preparing himself for their consumption.

Chad located the memo and scanned the text until he located the one line that proved his point. After making a copy, he grabbed a red marker and circled that line. He marched toward Sutton's office, waving the memo like a victory flag.

His sense of victory diminished when he discovered the lights were off and the door was locked.

Slightly disappointed that he could not have the face-to-face meeting he wanted, he began to sulk. Finally, he scribbled, "We did what you asked!" in the margin next to his red circle then slid the memo under the door, making sure it was face up.

Grinning at his triumph, he poked his head into Benton's office and boasted, "I'm going golfing, buddy. Have fun working."

Benton barely looked up. As his friend walked away pumping his fists, he shook his head and returned his attention to the proposal. He was immersed in his work and did not observe the alligator parade marching behind their victim.

Thirty minutes later, satisfied with the revisions, Benton delivered the revised proposal to Mr. Sutton, who had returned from the cafeteria.

Sutton motioned to a chair and asked him to wait while he read the changes. After a few moments he looked up. "Very good work. This is just what we needed. Thank you."

"Thanks," was all Benton could utter.

"Is Chad still here?"

Benton didn't want to hurt his friend, nor did he want to lie to his boss, so he hesitated a second before answering. "No. He left a little while ago."

Sutton rubbed his eyes and spoke slowly, in a weary voice, "Dan Skinner called as you two left. He wants to meet with me tonight instead of tomorrow morning. What he wants to know is how much money the new system will save him.

Fortunately, you have that well documented. I really appreciate how quickly you were able to make the changes. You probably know that Chad found the memo, and he is right. I made an error in the assignment. I wanted the product description and the client benefits, but didn't check the memo before I gave it to you two. I appreciate you staying here and correcting my error. Thanks to you, I can deliver this to him tonight ,and that should cement the deal."

"Glad I could help. I know how important this account is to us," Benton felt flush with excitement.

"Did Chad help or did you complete this by yourself?"

Benton looked away, then directly at his boss. He took a deep breath. "By myself. I knew we had to make the revisions, so I worked on it while Chad was locating the memo." He was proud of his work, yet embarrassed for his coworker.

Sutton smiled. "You have a very mature attitude and a solid work ethic. Based on your work, I think you understand this project better than anyone else. Can you meet with me tomorrow morning at eight o'clock to discuss how we can implement your ideas?"

Benton beamed. "Yes, I can. Thank you."

Sutton stood and shook Benton's hand. "Great. Get some rest and we'll get the project rolling tomorrow."

The next morning, Chad waltzed into his office and discovered two e-mails from Mr. Sutton in his PC mailbox. The first was only three words: "Please see me." The other was titled "Reorganization" and announced the promotion of Benton Williams to Project Manager for Skinner Construction projects.

As a less-confident Chad plodded toward the boss's office, he had the oddest sensation. He felt as if a fork had been thrust into his midsection.

In the gators' minds, he was done.

Chad makes several mistakes. First, he wastes time proving the boss wrong. Next, he fails to realize the mission had changed slightly.

Don't Tick Off the Gators!   51

He saves the dumbest mistake for last: he doesn't complete the work but leaves to play golf.

Chad chooses to dig deeper; Benton decides to dig out.

Chad invites the gators into his life and provides them a delicious, self-cooked meal. Wasting time proving the boss wrong is a big mistake and he compounds it with his arrogant message.

What does he gain by finding the boss's original memo and the error? What does he lose by writing the arrogant message?

Upon finding the original memo, Chad should do the mature thing. He should put it aside and work with Benton to revise the proposal to the new specifications. To Chad, however, it is more important to be right than to be productive.

Conversely, Benton focuses his attention on getting the work completed when the mission changes. His dedication pays off handsomely.

Before you use the shovel to damage yourself and your career, take a few minutes to weigh what you can gain from your actions and what you can lose. This is no time to win a minor skirmish at the cost of losing the campaign.

Thanks to Chad, this round goes to the gators!

EIGHT

Find the Gators Another Source of Food

You are an intelligent human being, capable of sound reasoning and logical thought processes. This gives you an advantage over a cold-blooded animal. So use it. Can the gators feast on something else instead of you?

A word of caution before you offer up your competition: never sacrifice another human being to advance your career or cause. It is a morally reprehensible act. No one will respect you if you sacrifice an innocent person to save your hide.

Do not blame the steno pool for failing to type your memo on time or the mail clerk for not delivering the FedEx package to you the minute it arrived. Be a man or woman of integrity. Hold yourself accountable for failure just as readily as you would accept the credit for success. Such a high level of integrity will gain you scores of admirers.

If there is a valid reason for not completing an assignment, such as the delivery service losing the CD you needed to complete a computer upgrade, or a trucker's strike in New Jersey, state the facts. Tell the truth and offer a solution when you present the problem.

If the gators can be distracted, then either distract them yourself or find a distraction. In a real-life game of survival, it is perfectly acceptable to point the alligators in the direction of small prey—especially if the gators intend to dine immediately.

> Jake Baylor stared in disbelief at the numbers on the computer screen. The income projection for Silver and Scout Horse Farms was $200,000 below the budget. As chief financial officer, he had the unenviable task of explaining that discrepancy to the board of directors.
>
> When Arthur Fox retired six months ago for health reasons, Jake was promoted to CFO. After three years as the vice president of finance, he was well versed in the corporation's financial position and philosophy. Although he didn't possess an accounting degree, he had an MBA and was respected for successfully managing the accounting operations. The board felt he was the ideal candidate based on his dedication, honesty, and professional management style.
>
> Jake could not understand the variance. It was illogical. How could a company that historically ran within two percent of income-and-budget projections have such a large discrepancy? He shook his head and began another systematic review of income statements.
>
> Engrossed in his work, he did not notice an eight-foot alligator crawl into the corner of his office. Nor did he sense the gator's stare.
>
> Jake reinserted the corporate budget CD-ROM and began a third review of the financials. After forty-five minutes of checking and cross checking, he found the problem.
>
> Gross revenue was predicated upon selling the Ohio properties for $7.5 million. The sale, however, booked on December 31, with revenue deferred until the current year, was for $7.1 million. Silver and Scout began the year with a $400,000 revenue deficit. "How did that happen?" he wondered.
>
> The gator stirred slightly, slapped his huge tail against the wall, and closed his eyes. He appeared to be asleep, but remained intent on devouring Jake.

Don't Tick Off the Gators! 55

Jake was glad he discovered the problem, but doing so caused an uncomfortable feeling that he couldn't shake. He knew he needed more information before he presented his findings to the board. The property sale information was a good start, but he wondered if other projections or calculations were also incorrect.

The gator continued to sleep, dreaming about his next meal and hoping it was soon.

You may only get one chance to distract the gators. Use it to your advantage.

Jake spent the evening developing a plan to review the budget and the property sale. The next morning he asked Laura Anson and Ben Van Meter to review the monthly variance reports, focusing on any ten-percent discrepancy. If they found one, it needed to be researched and explained in detail by noon.

That afternoon he completed his board report, using the information Laura and Ben had provided as support documentation.

The gator began to think that Jake might escape; that displeased him and made him edgy.

Jake's report to the board was characteristically succinct. He discussed the revenue discrepancy and the subsequent monthly variances that he attributed to it. He presented the facts without blaming anyone, especially Arthur Fox.

While he couldn't explain the difference between the projected sales price and the actual price, he was not going to blame Arthur Fox. Jake had worked closely with Arthur on the budget and knew his predecessor was too conservative to inflate the projected revenue from the sale.

Everett McClain, Chairman of the Finance Committee, was the first to speak "Thank you, Jake, another excellent report."

Clearing his throat and looking around the room, he went on, "There is a reason for the difference. We—that is the board— reduced the price at a special meeting before Christmas to

> complete the sale by December thirty-first. The board is at fault for not reporting this to you earlier."
> As Everett droned on, Jake sat silently and felt the tension fade. He was relieved that he and Arthur were not at fault. Too relieved to be angry at the board.
> Jake's gator slithered off, looking for easier prey.

Jake Baylor conducts himself professionally and honorably; he refuses to blame an innocent man. Instead of sacrificing his predecessor, he looks for the cause of the problem and directs the gators away from himself.

Jake never intends to ruin the reputation of his predecessor and friend. Once he finds the revenue shortfall, he tells the truth and does not try to sacrifice someone else. Making the problem the focus of his investigation, not Arthur Fox, Jake does more than solve a problem; he also reveals the depth of his character.

NINE

Change the Mission and Save Limbs

In a crisis you have an excellent opportunity to learn if you will react in a manner that preserves both your dignity and career. If you solve the problem, what will you gain? If you fail, what will you lose?

Homer Bonds started to sweat ice-cold pellets at exactly nine fifteen. That was the moment Interstate Delivery Service's distribution manager informed him that they could not locate a package he expected. Interstate confirmed that it was shipped two days ago but had no idea where it was now.

He needed that package. It contained a set of electronic controls he needed to finish a security system for Atlas Warehouse. Without the controls, he would lose the contract.

Homer called the supplier, asking them to send a replacement, but that proved fruitless, as well. His order was custom-built, and they needed at least three days to manufacture a replacement.

Atlas selected him, a local contractor, over several better-known firms, because a friend went to bat for him. His high school buddy, Stan Robinson, an Atlas executive, had personally vouched for his ability to deliver a quality system on time.

Homer knew he had to do something. No amount of yelling or swearing was going to change the fact that the package was lost. He grabbed a Diet Coke from his refrigerator and sat down to think.

Two rather large gators made their way into his office and found a comfortable spot to wait for their dinner, just behind the workbench.

He spoke aloud to himself, "I have two choices: find replacement parts or come up with a way to secure the building until I get the parts."

He took several swigs, then started smiling. He had an idea. Leaning back in his chair, Homer began to plot his strategy.

The gators smiled bemusedly at each other and continued their vigil.

Once he was convinced he had a plan, Homer called Stan and asked what time he could begin installing the system.

"Any time after six. The security guard is expecting you and will let you in."

"Thanks, we'll be there just after six."

Homer loaded his van for the night's work and made one last call to Interstate Delivery. Using their electronic tracing system, he learned the package had been located and would be delivered by ten—tomorrow morning.

Punching numbers quickly, he transferred to the dispatch office and requested they deliver it to the Atlas Warehouse. After some tedious verification procedures, the dispatcher agreed and gave him a new confirmation number.

Homer left messages for his two part-time employees, telling them to meet him at five thirty. Then he headed home for a nap. He would need it.

The gators were not sure what was going on. They joined Homer in the van and wondered if dinner might not be a sure thing.

Arriving at Atlas just after six, the three men carried their equipment and electronic components into the warehouse.

They began work at six-thirty and worked without a break for over four hours. A few minutes after eleven, they completed the wiring and testing. The tests were positive, and they decided to take a break.

Homer smiled, knowing he was almost done. All they needed to do was install the controls and control panel. "Boys, the control sensors didn't arrive today. They'll be here tomorrow morning."

Foster and Grant stared at him. Finally, Grant spoke, "Then why did we work tonight?"

"Atlas was promised a security system tonight. They got it."

"It doesn't work."

"No, but I do. I'll stay here tonight and make sure no one gets in. You two can go home, but meet me here at nine forty-five tomorrow morning. We'll finish it then."

Foster and Grant shrugged and headed for the exit.

Homer walked out to the security gate to inform the guard he would remain in the building all night. "I need to monitor the system and don't want to leave it unsupervised overnight."

Minutes later he climbed onto a catwalk with a view of the entire warehouse. He had large Thermos of coffee, a radio, and the latest Stephen Coonts novel. Atlas Warehouse was secure, outside, under the watchful eyes of a security guard, and it was secured inside by Homer Bonds.

The angry gators crawled into a vacant storage unit, knowing their next meal would be breakfast, not a midnight snack.

The next morning Foster and Grant arrived and found their boss in Stan Robinson's office. The two old friends were drinking coffee and, as usual, were discussing baseball.

Homer waved for them to enter. He offered them coffee and switched the conversation to business. "Stan, once the package arrives, I can upgrade your system from manual to automatic. We'll demonstrate the procedures to your people and be out of your way by eleven."

Robinson asked, "Any problems last night?"

"Just one," Homer replied with a smile, "but I spent the night here to make sure your warehouse was secure. It was then and will be from now on."

"I knew you could do it."

"Thanks for the opportunity, old friend. I'd better get out of your way and let you get some work done."

Foster and Grant stared at their boss then followed him to the control panel.

The parts arrived as scheduled. Homer, Foster, and Grant installed the controls and completed the job as promised. When Homer was satisfied that the Atlas employees understood the operations, he packed his gear and was on the road ten minutes before eleven.

As he backed his van out of the parking the space, he thought he saw two alligators climb into the cab of an Interstate Delivery truck. He figured his brain was playing tricks on him due to lack of sleep.

Homer keeps his word and delivers a security system on time. He arrives at an alternate solution and makes sure the friend who hired him doesn't join him on the chopping block.

Homer changes the mission slightly and leaves unscathed.

Disappointed gators have to search for other prey.

TEN

What Would McGyver Do?

Is it time to be daring and devise a creative solution? Angus McGyver, of the '80s ABC television show *McGyver*, escapes from countless predicaments by applying his considerable scientific knowledge and creative genius. He uses the resources at hand to knock down doors, escape from confinement, and repair seeming useless vehicles. Some viewers may laugh at his methods, but the underlying message is that, by thinking beyond the obvious, McGyver can turn ordinary items into useful tools. You can do the same thing.

Okay, you may not blow down a door using PVC pipe, a sack of flour, a length of twine, and a candle. But you are an expert in your field and possess the ability to think beyond surface level. You can solve your problems by creatively using the resources at hand.

> Winthrop Grich marched confidently into the conference room, prepared to market his company's data security services to Grayson, West, & Gordon. Landing the city's most prestigious law firm would not only add to his standing within the

company, but the residual bonuses would fatten his bank account for years.

Winthrop opened his briefcase and withdrew a stack of bound handouts, his meticulous notes, a CD-ROM containing the presentation, and his trusty laser pointer. He was ready.

One by one, the managing partners arrived and either shook his hand or nodded before sitting in their assigned seats. Finally, James Andrew McGregor, the managing partner, entered and sat at the head of the table, in the biggest chair.

"Win," he began, "we asked you here to talk to us about data security, which we need, without any doubt. But this morning I saw a report on CNN that, to be frank, scared me to death. The report indicated that most companies do not have a disaster recovery or business continuity plan. I asked our data people about our plan, and to my dismay, they told me that we don't have one. Can you help us with that?"

Win stared at the group of attorneys and uttered a confident, "Yes, sir."

No sooner had the words escaped his lips than a gang of teenage gators, clad in black leather and biker hats, strutted into the room and defiantly surrounded him.

What the gators and the attorneys fail to observe is Winthrop's mind kicking into high gear. He is having a "McGyver moment" and is ready to blow the hinges off this trap.

Mr. McGregor may attempt to make him squirm, but he is asking Winthrop for help. Winthrop remains poised and decides to let the attorneys stew a bit. Then he will offer to design and implement a business continuity plan for them.

In this type of situation it is imperative to think first and speak second. Too many people exacerbate a crisis by speaking before completing the thought process. You need to understand the situation before you speak, especially if you say that you will solve the problem.

Think carefully about your plan, make sure it works, then take action. If you need an extraordinary solution, follow McGyver's example:

- Assess the situation
- Think beyond the most obvious and immediate answer
- Apply your knowledge
- Use the resources at hand—quickly

You are in crisis mode. If a solution isn't obvious, it is time to be creative.

Winthrop reached into his briefcase and retrieved a legal pad. He took a deep breath and looked around the room. Confident that he possessed a solution, he asked, "Ladies and gentlemen, how long would it take to duplicate every paper and electronic file in this firm?"

From around the table came a variety of answers—none stated with assurance. Most were guesses, ranging from months to years.

"How would you do it, and how much would it cost?"

A few attorneys shifted nervously. Winthrop knew he had them, but wanted to make them even more nervous.

"How would you conduct business if your computer system was destroyed by a hacker or a worm?"

The anxiety heightened. One more question and they would open their personal checkbooks, begging him for an answer.

He paused for effect and then spoke quietly, "How soon do you need to develop a comprehensive business continuity and data security plan? One that covers you from data entry to data storage and through an unforeseen disaster recovery?"

McGregor stared at Winthrop, and said grimly, "Today."

Winthrop met the senior man's eyes with a smile, "Then let's get started."

He handed McGregor a copy of the presentation and circled the room, handing one to each partner. McGregor flipped to the "Executive Summary" and began reading. The other partners followed his lead.

After examining the document carefully and thinking for a few minutes, McGregor looked around the room, making eye contact with each partner. He spun his chair toward Winthrop and broke the silence. "This proposal addresses my concerns. Your company appears to possess the ability to help us protect our data and intellectual assets. Based on this proposal, you are telling me you can begin work once the contracts are signed. Is that a fair representation of the facts?"

Winthrop nodded, "Yes, sir. We can begin work as soon as the ink is dry."

"If you can add a section that addresses data recovery in terms more specific to our practice, then you are hired. That is, barring any dissent from this committee, which I do not expect."

The other partners bobbed their heads automatically and quickly. There was no dissent.

McGregor rose and shook Winthrop's hand. "Have your attorney fax me a contract with the new language—today." Then he strode out of the conference room.

One by one, the other attorneys exited, leaving Winthrop alone with a stunned and satisfied look on his face.

The alligators were dazed; their intended meal vanished before their eyes. Even worse, attorneys now protected him. These young alligator hoods knew they were no match for professionals and decided to harass the IT department on the way out, just for laughs.

Winthrop escapes from the gators by using his knowledge and the resources at hand, just like Angus McGyver.

He uses the fears of Grayson, West, & Gordon as his lever. The law firm is afraid of lost data and lost business continuity. Winthrop turns that into his advantage and lands the big account.

Like McGyver, you too may need to improvise and use the available tools. Apply your knowledge, experience, or the experiences handed to you by others to solve your problems. Use your mind and the available resources to escape the gators. Think beyond the obvious and find a solution that less creative people miss.

ELEVEN

If You Have Weapons, Use Them Wisely

If you face more than one gator, you need to slow down the entire pack. Start with the leader. Shooting the most aggressive gator will cause the others to hesitate. Six well-placed bullets can eliminate an equal number of gators and scatter the remainder. Use your weapons wisely to frighten the gators.

Firing warning shots into the air only works on scripted TV police shows, not in real life. Your goal is to solve a problem. Do that instead of wasting time in pointless activity.

Don't waste your time, your employees, or the time of others in fruitless efforts. If your deadline is imminent, invest your time and resources well. Don't waste bullets.

> Bascombe Carlton steered his car into a parking space at Theodore and Williams. Before exiting, he rehearsed his sales pitch a final time. He reminded himself to emphasize the key points: the long-range savings of his company's payroll software and the ease of automatic record data storage. Surely a big company with multi-state operations could use a modern and efficient payroll system.

He was quaking inside. He hadn't closed a deal in weeks, his boss was riding him big time, and he was beginning to feel the financial pinch. He was also certain that he smelled alligators nearby.

As he sat in the company's finance center lobby, Bascombe overheard a conversation between two men dressed in dark blue "T & W" uniforms. Based on the discussion, he ascertained that they were delivery men.

The taller man spoke angrily, saying, "They still haven't gotten my paycheck right. For three months now, I've been paid at the old rate. Every time I talk to that Colavito character, he brushes me off with, 'We'll get it fixed, and you won't lose any money. Be patient.'"

For no apparent reason, the pair stopped walking and stood right in front of Bascombe, and he heard each word clearly.

"Funny, he never even asks me what the problem is. Just gives me a patronizing answer. I'm tired of being patient, I want my money—now," said one.

"I know what you mean. I have the same problem," his friend replied. "They *seem* to listen, but they don't *seem* to care. Maybe they're busy fixing a lot of errors. We can't be the only guys whose checks are messed up."

"I don't really care about anyone else. I just want them to get ours right. If we screwed up our deliveries like they do our paychecks, we'd be gone by now," the first man answered.

The second man grunted his agreement.

As the two men walked away and out the door, Bascombe Carlton smiled. This is the break I've been looking for, he thought.

Bascombe, recognizing the value of what he heard, took a moment to decide how to use this information in his sales pitch. The proper sequence of questions and statements became clear. He had his plan.

Not just a plan, but leverage in the form of employees unhappy because their paychecks were not correct. That was something no company wanted. He remembered the taller man's name—Crandall. Bascombe scribbled a few notes onto his presentation pad and silently rehearsed his revised spiel. Confident that he was ready, he relaxed.

As he did, the gators, who covertly followed him into the building, looked at each other. They hoped Bascombe's celebration was premature, since they considered him "a sure thing."

Bascombe sat and leafed through *Smithsonian* Magazine. Twenty minutes later, he walked to the water fountain, took a drink, and looked around the lobby.

Before long, Clyde Weaver, payroll director, ambled toward him, extending his right hand. Clyde greeted him in staccato bursts. "Bascombe, thanks for coming today. I apologize for the delay. We're running way behind. It has been one of those days. Nothing has gone right since breakfast. I really should cancel the meeting, but since you came so far, we ought to give you the courtesy of hearing what you have to say."

"Mr. Weaver, nice to see you again. I'm sorry things aren't going well and appreciate your consideration. I promise to be brief and save you some time," Bascome answered.

"That would be great," he replied, ushering Bascombe through the corridor and into a small meeting room. The room was filled with stressed payroll managers. Their body language indicated that the last thing they wanted was to hear a sales pitch.

Taking a seat near the door, Bascombe did not see two alligators enter and position themselves by the drink table at the rear of the room.

"Ladies and gentlemen, Mr. Weaver told me that you are in a time crunch. I appreciate that and will not take up too much of your time."

A few appreciative remarks were made as he opened his binder and looked around the table.

Starting quickly, he spoke confidently. "How long does it take to implement a payroll change for a salaried employee?"

"Fifteen minutes," came from a cocky voice on the left side of the table.

"Okay. How often is it correct?"

"All the time!" the same voice answered.

Laughter erupted from the far corner. Weaver glanced sternly at them, and the laughter ceased.

"How about an hourly employee? For example, a delivery truck driver?"

"Excuse me, but where is this going?" barked Weaver.

Bascombe replied calmly, "Just trying to establish a baseline. I promise to be brief."

Sandra Allen answered, very quietly. "It takes a bit longer because we need to have hourly pay change forms signed by their immediate supervisor, the hourly payroll administrator, and the division vice president. It can take weeks."

"Actually, months," Bascombe stated with conviction, then continued. "Months because you have a complex, paper-based system. My software can change your paper-based system into a totally electronic system in a few weeks." He paused to let his comment sink in.

"I say months, not to embarrass you, Ms. Allen, but because two of your employees told me so—today." Again a strategic pause, greeted by dead silence.

"Ladies and gentlemen. I can fix that problem and others associated with paper forms by installing electronic workflow. Electronic forms will be automatically routed to the appropriate manager, allowing Mr. Weaver to know the status of *every* change. You will have virtually no delayed changes and very satisfied employees." Then he closed his binder, waiting for them to speak.

Clyde Weaver spoke first, angrily. "Who told you this? How would they know to tell *you*?"

Bascombe replied, "I overheard a conversation while sitting in the lobby. Do you have more than two employees with salary adjustment problems?"

Weaver stared at Bascombe, then looked at Sandy Allen and asked softly, "Do we, Sandy?"

"Yes, sir, we do."

Slightly chastened, Weaver turned to Bascombe, "Mr. Carlton, you made your point and quickly, as you promised.

The volume of paperwork around here is ridiculous and a hassle for my people. If you don't mind, Ms. Allen and I would like to meet with you to learn more about your solution. Unfortunately, we need to meet with the human resources vice president in ten minutes. Sandy and I will probably take a few bullets because of some of the issues you raised. Might help our case if we tell him that you can help us. Can you wait around and meet with us afterward?"

"Yes, sir. I'd be glad to."

"I thought you might. I can promise you our undivided attention at that time."

As the group walked out, Sandy Allen looked back and shot Bascombe an embarrassed, yet grateful smile.

The gators were disappointed that Bascombe escaped their clutches but decided to stick around Theodore and Williams. It appeared there would be some payroll manager flesh to gnaw on very soon.

When Bascombe Carlton hears Crandall and his co-worker discuss their paycheck problems, he is handed a weapon. The delivery men give him the information he needs to prove he can solve a big problem, as well as improve the payroll system. He uses that information, makes the sale, and escapes from the gators.

Use your weapons effectively. Aim your shots wisely.

TWELVE

Are the Gators More Afraid than You?

Probably not, but who knows?
Is the problem one you create, or does it arise from someone's fears? Think about the problem *and* its cause. Knowing the cause will help you solve the problem.

> Sid Belanger gazed distractedly out his office window. The overcast and drizzly day did nothing to lighten his mood. As he gazed, he boiled down the situation to its most basic element: "If I don't come up with an advertising campaign for R&R Publications, I am toast."
>
> As he sat looking into the distance, a small family of alligators found a cozy spot next to his conference table.
>
> Just fifteen minutes ago, R&R Publications, a longtime client, rejected his marketing ideas. To add to the pain of rejection, they threatened to "look for a fresher source" if he didn't "meet their needs" by tomorrow morning. R&R's rejection and threat had been pronounced in front of his boss, leading to a nuclear eruption.

For more time than Sid thought necessary, his boss, Rory Mathewson, blasted him with a tirade that included a threat "to draw and quarter him" if he didn't save this account. The words "draw and quarter" had been accompanied by a string of profanities that would embarrass a Longshoreman.

Rory's parting words still stung Sid. "If R&R walks, so do you!"

At times like this, it is necessary to step back, remove the emotion, and analyze the situation from another perspective. What is the cause of the problem? Once you identify the cause of a problem, it is much easier to solve.

Sid decided to take another look at what he had presented. He had offered his client a new, classier campaign. What was not to like? It was innovative, bold, and emphasized R&R's competitive prices and their status as solid members of the community. He highlighted the company's civic donations: sponsoring youth music competitions, bicycle races, and their annual blood drive.

He compared that with the advertising videos of R&R's main competition. *National Magazine Stand* was running another glitzy campaign, filled with voluptuous, bikini-clad women strutting on a beach, signing eager and gullible men to subscriptions.

Sid spoke to himself, "Very cliché. R&R wants something just like that, something that grabs the attention of men. It is as if they want to play follow the leader."

His words caused him to sit up straight. He continued talking aloud to himself, "R&R doesn't want an original idea; they want to outdo *National Magazine Stand* at whatever *National* does. They didn't like my ideas because they want to duplicate *National Magazine Stand*.

Suddenly his brain was full of ideas. He spun in his chair and began pounding on the keyboard. Sid was locked into a single train of thought, creating a new PowerPoint presentation for his clients. He thought, An idea that will work, if not for them, then for a client with more guts.

Don't Tick Off the Gators! 73

Sid worked nonstop for three hours. Once he was satisfied, he called it a day. "A very good day, Sid," he said to himself and, unknowingly, to the family of gators.

The following morning Sid arrived at seven thirty to prepare the conference room for his meeting with R&R. After starting the coffeemaker and arranging a tray of doughnuts in the center of the table, he placed a small device in the chair to his immediate right.

Roland Scioscia and Ralph Baker, dressed in matching khaki slacks and navy "R&R Pubs" polo shirts, arrived at eight-fifteen, accompanied by a very tense Rory Mathewson.

Skipping the pleasantries, the three men poured their own coffee and grabbed doughnuts before sitting across from Sid.

"Let's see what you got, big boy," Baker barked.

Sid offered a mischievous smile and turned on the LCD projector. Leaning very surreptitiously to his right, he activated the machine he had secreted on the chair next to him.

"Gentlemen, here is the future advertising campaign for R&R," he began confidently.

"Yes, sir! Great job, sir! You are the man!" cried out a cheery voice from the chair.

Baker, Scioscia, and Mathewson looked from one to another in confusion.

Sid continued, suppressing a laugh, "As, I was saying—"

"Great idea! Pure genius! I love it!" the machine crowed.

"What are you up to, Sid?" demanded an outraged Mathewson.

"Wonderful idea, the best yet!" it continued.

"Cut it out. Are you insane?" Mathewson reddened.

"Amazing! Inspired! A Winner!" it crescendoed.

Sid reached over and turned off the machine. At first he wondered if he had crossed the line, then he realized he didn't care.

"Gentlemen, this is 'The Yes Man.'" he announced, as he handed the human-shaped machine to Scioscia.

"The Yes Man will always tell you how smart and wonderful you are. He will stroke your ego all day. However, he will not tell you the truth."

Pausing to look at each man for effect, he continued, "If you want The Yes Man, he's yours. He will tell you how smart you are whenever you want him to. But if you want a new advertising campaign—one that distinguishes you from *National Magazine Stand*—then you need to listen to me."

Baker and Scioscia locked eyes, then both men nodded in Sid's direction.

"Go ahead," said Scioscia.

Sid enthusiastically explained his idea for a four-month campaign of new ads. Each designed to demonstrate a difference between R&R and *National Magazine Stand*.

One ad focused on their excellent reputation for customer service, another revolved around competitive pricing, while a third stressed their wide range of books, magazines, and other publications. The last was designed for the holiday season. Each ad, whether in print, on radio or television, included a reference to their community involvement.

Baker and Scioscia warmed to the plan. Reluctantly, they admitted that it was easier to mirror *National Magazine Stand* than to try a different approach.

"Their success, unfortunately, is a misconception. Market research indicates that women and the more conservative members of the community are offended by the bikini ads. Your campaign to demonstrate a difference in values will win you those market shares," Sid explained.

As Sid wrapped up the deal, the gators crawled out, angry and still hungry. They thought about attacking Rory but decided that he might be too tough for the younger ones to chew.

Sid Belanger separates his emotions from the situation, gains a clear view of the problem, and finds a way to solve it. He tries a bold, offbeat idea, and it works. When you have little to lose, fear is not a deterrent to acting boldly.

When he identifies the real problem—R&R's fear of being different than their competition—he uses his creative talents to expose that fear. Sid's clever use of the "The Yes Man" breaks the tension and demonstrates his point with humor.

When you overcome your fear, you can exploit the gator's fear. You may only have one opportunity to succeed. Take advantage of it.

Out wait them or out wit them. Sid out wits the gators by using his brains, his sense of humor, and his guts. He leaves the swamp with a victory.

THIRTEEN

*How Did This Happen?
Can I Prevent It in the Future?*

A crisis is not the time for self-flagellation; there are enough people on the sidelines willing to take swings at you. A more beneficial approach is to perform a battlefield assessment.

It is time for an honest review of the events that placed you in the swamp. You may discover the solution to your problem or learn how to prevent the mistake from reoccurring in the future. Optimally, you will do both.

> Seth Warner couldn't believe it had happened again; but once again his management meeting disintegrated into a verbal brawl.
>
> As operations manager for Watson and Holmes, a business supply company, he chaired the weekly meeting of six department heads. The meeting was designed to provide a management vehicle to correct problems in their infancy, promote cooperation, and ensure that company policies were followed throughout the organization. In reality, it was a breeding ground for internal bickering and hostility.

In each of the last four weeks, the meeting deteriorated into a series of nasty verbal exchanges. Distribution attacked warehousing. warehousing attacked information systems. All three attacked sales, but for different reasons. Accounting complained about late payments from clients, and that agitated everyone.

Alone in his office, Seth launched a mental replay of today's meeting. He realized that things went south when he asked, "Does anyone have any pressing issues?"

While he stared at the wall, four small but aggressive young gators entered his office and parked behind his chair, waiting for their next meal.

After making a note on a legal pad, he retrieved his management meeting file. Seth examined the notes he had written on agendas for the previous weeks and discovered the common point of breakdown—it happened each time he asked for comments or updates from his managers. From there, the meeting rapidly became a finger-pointing and argument session.

He walked to his bookshelf and located a small paperback book about conflict management. Seth returned to his desk and reread items he'd highlighted in yellow many years ago. Even with timeworn Hi-Liter marks, he could still detect the points he considered important when he first read the book. Today their message remained abundantly clear.

Seth identified the recurring problem by taking a few minutes to think about the events that triggered the outbreaks. Then he used a resource, the conflict management book, to help solve the problem.

Seth quickly developed a meeting agenda then sent a high priority email to his managers, asking them to meet him at nine the next morning.

When the managers arrived in the conference room, they noticed an easel in one corner of the room. On it was printed three words: Fix It Together.

Seth was the last to arrive and spoke as he entered the room. "People, your behavior at the last four management meetings has been unprofessional, unacceptable, and unproductive. The only thing worse has been my failure to stop it. I'm correcting *my* mistake right now. Together we will use this meeting to begin correcting *your* behavior."

"Hold on," blurted Maynard Evans, the distribution manager. Seth cut him off with the wave of his hand. "I'm establishing some new rules for this meeting. The first is that there will be no discussion about the past meetings. Right now, I need for each of you to *listen*. Your turn to talk will come later. Management meetings were designed to help us address issues critical to the operations of Watson and Holmes. We must be able to discuss problems and challenges without rancor, without finger pointing, and without egos being damaged. Retaliation is not a solution."

Walking around the table, he handed each manager a sheet of paper. "You will each spend a half day with the other departments, as indicated on this schedule. No exceptions, no excuses. You *will* do it. We'll meet again Monday to discuss what you learned. Any questions?"

Maynard, still seething about being cut off, shot out, "I have a meeting with the truck drivers at the same time you have me scheduled for accounting."

"Change your drivers' meeting. This schedule will be followed as indicated. No exceptions. Does anyone else have anything to say?"

When nobody spoke, Seth smiled. "Thanks. Have fun." He walked out, ignoring his manager's grumbling comments.

Seth's plan was to have his managers walk a mile in each other's moccasins. They needed to learn how each department fit into the overall operations, their interdependence, and to understand the challenges the other managers faced.

Monday, Seth purposely delayed his arrival for the management meeting by ten minutes, hoping the managers would use the time to bond.

"Okay, people. Today's agenda is a short one. I need to leave for another meeting in forty-five minutes. We'll go around the table, and everyone gets one minute to tell the status of his or her department. Maynard?"

Maynard thought for a moment and said, "We are one day behind on shipping, but we'll be caught up by Friday. Seems the warehouse had—"

Seth stopped him in mid-sentence. "Limit your remarks to only your area. Corey can speak for the warehouse."

Disgustedly, Maynard said, "Then I have nothing else to add."

"Cassandra, you're next. What is new in support?"

"Seth, we're finally caught up on the backlog of orders. Jarvis and the accounting staff were a big help." Cassandra Wells smiled, glad she had something positive to contribute.

"Jarvis, before your head swells, what is accounting doing?" Seth began to think his idea might work.

"We are working on the past-due accounts this week," responded Jarvis Witt. "Let me add that Dana and the sales staff helped us sort out some older accounts and called some of the more difficult clients for us."

Seth nodded. "Corey?"

Corey Osteen looked around the room before he spoke. "Seth, we just cannot get the orders out to Maynard fast enough. My staff is working like crazy, but we can't keep up with the volume."

"Not a bad problem to have. We'll come back to that in minute."

"Dana?"

"My people," she said pointedly toward Corey, "are hearing lots of complaints about the orders being late. We're selling like crazy but slow deliveries are hurting repeat business."

Seth wanted to prevent any angry replies, so he interjected, "Dana, when your people a promise a delivery date, do they check with Corey or Maynard to make sure it can be delivered as promised?"

"No, they don't check with anyone. How would that make them look to the client?"

As noise around the table grew, Seth inquired, "Would they look any worse than when they have to explain why the order is late?"

Dana Parks flashed Seth an irritated look. "No," she admitted.

"We'll come back to that issue in a minute. Therese?"

Therese Roseboro, information systems manager, responded, "The network is running smoothly. Knock on wood. The new computers will be configured by Thursday, and I'll send out an installation schedule early next week."

Seth looked at each manager and smiled. "Was that so difficult? To just listen to the others and not get into a cat fight?"

Sheepish grins came from all but Maynard and Dana.

"Now we have two issues to solve. One, the matter of how and when we schedule deliveries. Two, when we can install new terminals."

"Maynard and Dana. I want the two of you to schedule time, together with Therese, to review the new scheduling software. By this time next week, I want you two managers to have a resolution to this delivery problem.

"Therese, you will need to schedule the installations on a department-by-department basis. Please prioritize the schedule to keep downtime and work interruptions to a minimum. I will defer to your judgment on prioritization and scheduling. If your people need flex time or overtime to meet that schedule, make sure Jarvis is aware of it for payroll purposes.

"Ladies and gentlemen," he continued, "Is there anyone who felt the cross exposure to the other departments was a waste of time?"

Maynard and Dana both spoke up at once, "Yes."

Not surprised by their answer, Seth asked, "Dana, why do you feel that way?"

"I needed to resolve the late deliveries, not watch the truck drivers loading trucks."

"I needed to help my guys, not listen to her sales force on the phone," growled Maynard.

"Anyone else?"

Jarvis broke an uncomfortable silence. "Seth, I think your point was that none of us truly understands the interactions of and with the other departments. We all got the message." Looking from Dana to Maynard he added, "Even those two."

Dana blurted, "Listen, mister, I do not need your—"

"ENOUGH!" Seth's command was followed by dead silence.

Slowly Seth regained his self-control and continued, "That type of outburst is no longer acceptable, Dana. From you or anyone else." He scanned the room. "We are adults, professionals. We *will* act like it. Dana, you and Maynard need to end this feud. He can't fill the orders as fast as you are selling. Maynard, your people need to pick up the pace. I suggest that you two *adults* start communicating better—right now. Your inability to work together is hurting Watson and Holmes. I shouldn't have to say this, but your communication problems better not cost us so much as *one* client."

Both managers glared at Seth and then, realizing he was right, looked away.

Glancing around the room, Seth added, "That last statement could have been directed to any of you in the last four weeks. Today Dana and Maynard—and to some extent Jarvis—caught it for all of your past behaviors. Problems have to be solved and arguing doesn't solve them. Working together does."

As the meeting continued, the four gators decided to split up. Two would follow Dana, one would follow Maynard, and one crept up behind Jarvis. Oddly, gators like hard heads; it must be the challenge of biting through a thick skull.

Seth Warner identifies the problem and isolates the behaviors that lead to his management team's arguing and finger pointing. Seth takes action to prevent a reoccurrence and starts driving the gators away from his management team. He also removes them from his life.

Remember: When enemies surround you, be your own best friend.

FOURTEEN

Stop Shaking—It Doesn't Help

To control a situation, you must first control yourself.
Shaking, anger, tears, yelling, and expressing fear do not solve a problem. Put your emotions aside so you can think logically and calmly. After the triumph, you can allow your emotions to circle the bases. For now, just be cool.

In a crisis, you need to think clearly and develop a plan. Concentrate on solving the problem and completing the mission. Everything else is a distraction and waste of time and resources.

> Chantal Welch, Ph.D., was petrified at the thought of addressing the convention. Just three days ago she learned the expected speaker, a highly regarded expert on the convention's central theme of "Nontraditional Business Curriculum", had cancelled because of a family illness. Yesterday, to her chagrin, the National Business College Convention's education committee selected her to fill the vacancy.
>
> Looking for a controversial subject, the committee asked her to discuss the curriculum dispute that rocked her small

Midwestern school two years ago. As the dean of Sisler Business College, she had been embroiled in a battle over the requirement that all MBA students pass the corporate ethics course prior to graduation.

Her staunchest opponent, then and now, was Professor Winston Anderson, postgraduate curriculum advisor. He maintained that ethics was a personal choice and, as such, Sisler could mandate neither the course nor the necessity to pass it.

After several months of heated arguments, turmoil-filled board meetings, and negative publicity, Professor Anderson had resigned "on principle." He continued the fight by attacking Chantal whenever he was interviewed or wrote for professional journals.

Chantal won the fight, but it was costly. Students and staff viewed her decision with skepticism. Some felt she was openly accusing them of having no ethics, while others felt it was a power play to oust Professor Anderson. Yet another group thought she overstepped her authority in making ethics a required course.

As Chantal pondered the curriculum fight and the upcoming speech, two rather tough-looking alligators made themselves at home in the living area of her hotel suite.

Professor Welch faces a common fear, the fear of public speaking. Although she is a highly regarded and successful professional, she is not comfortable speaking to a crowd. She prefers conducting conversations with small groups of graduate students, as opposed to giving lectures.

Overcoming this anxiety is not easy; it requires time and great effort. Most people avoid situations requiring them to address crowds. Some people, like Chantal, are forced to speak, regardless of their fear. Horrified or not, they must speak.

Chantal wasn't sure where to start, what to say, or how to properly address the subject. Furthermore, she knew Winston Anderson would attend the opening session. She decided that the pompous jerk would probably sit in the front row to try and intimidate her. Nothing that ran through her mind gave her comfort.

Ideas were not flowing, at least not as freely as the stress, so she decided to go for a run in the late afternoon air and clear her head.

While running along the river, she recalled the reasons she insisted on the ethics course. The proliferation of companies facing accounting and management issues bothered her deeply. Business and public trust should be linked.

But with the problems at Enron, Arthur Andersen, Tyco, and a host of other corporations being covered in the news media, someone needed to take a stand and effect a change. She didn't want Sisler graduates entering the business world without understanding the need for corporate ethics.

As she ran, her intended message became clear and the speech began to write itself. By the time she finished running, Chantal sensed an opportunity to present her ideas forcefully and without interruption.

After showering, she sat at the desk and typed her thoughts into her laptop. Working at a controlled pace, she organized them into a logical sequence. Within the hour, she was satisfied with the results.

Now all she had to do was stand at the podium tomorrow and deliver it. The thing she feared most.

The two gators made threatening gestures with their stubby front legs and flashed their teeth.

Chantal clears her mind and solves a portion of her problem—what to say. Now that the speech is written, she must deliver it. As uncomfortable as that makes her feel, she knows what she has to say is important—too important to allow her fear to stop her from expressing her views to the convention.

Large problems can be broken into smaller ones. Smaller ones are easier to solve and give you the confidence to tackle the larger ones.

That evening, Chantal dined with her closest friend, Crystal O'Malley. She and Crystal had been friends since they met in the Business School Library at Stanford. While Chantal chose academia, Crystal became an investment banker.

Over a glass of cabernet, she related her fear of public speaking. "I wish I could find a way to relax. I'm nervous before the speech, but once I get to the podium, it's worse. I literally freeze up. My knees knock, my throat tightens, I feel overwhelmed, and I just want to disappear."

Crystal sipped her wine and smiled empathetically. "What you describe is normal. I get that way all the time, except instead of knocking knees, my hands shake visibly. I can't even *think* about holding a glass of water!"

Chantal was stunned and stared at her friend. "Really? I never would have guessed that. How do you hide it so well?"

Crystal giggled, then smiled coyly. "Talking to stuffed shirts about their potential return on investment is not easy. I have to divert my attention from the audience and just let it flow. You remember the old advice about imagining your audience naked or naked except for black socks?"

"Yes. Seems silly," Chantal admitted.

"It is. Besides, Winston Anderson will be in the front row, and I don't think you want *that* picture in your mind!"

They both shuddered at the thought of the corpulent professor in the buff, with or without black socks. Then they laughed.

"Seriously, what works for me is to remember the eighty-twenty rule," Crystal explained. "Face it, eighty percent of the audience isn't listening. They're thinking about the flight home, their dinner plans, their kids, or whatever. The ones who *are* listening—the twenty percent—think you're a genius and will hang onto your every word. Aim for them. They're easy to spot, because they're actually looking at you. It's in their eyes. You can see that they're hungry for your knowledge."

"You make it sound so easy,"Chantal sighed. "I never liked this aspect of my profession. One on one I'm fine, but addressing a crowd, well, it isn't my idea of fun."

"That is exactly what I'm telling you. Find a person who is listening and make eye contact. Talk to him or her. Then find another one and another. Keep searching the audience for kind eyes and hungry eyes, lock on them and talk to the face behind the eyes. Trust me on this, it works every time."

Reaching across the table for her friend's hand, Crystal continued, "Tomorrow you will be awesome. Start by looking at me, like I'm the only person in the room. I'll be in the third row on the center aisle. Then look behind me for another set of kind eyes and keep doing that. Before you know it, you will be finished."

As they completed dinner, Chantal's mind drifted away from her speech and to her key lime pie.

The gators were not pleased and looked around the room for a drunk or obnoxious boor to hassle. Chantal did not seem like such a sure thing anymore.

The next morning Chantal sat alone in her room thinking about what her friend said. *It cannot hurt to try Crystal's idea. Look for kind and hungry eyes.*

She rehearsed one final time, directing her remarks to the talking face on CNN. Chantal relaxed. A smile crept across her face and then vanished. The trepidation was still there. So was the thought of pompous Winston Anderson mocking her from his seat in the front row.

The gators began to fidget. Professor Welch might be fair game after all.

The long wait passed, and Chantal found herself standing in the wings, repeating, "This is an important message, people want to hear it." Mentally, she checked off the key elements of her speech, trying not to listen to the moderator as he droned on.

When he finished extolling the extensive credentials and accomplishments of "the noted Doctor Chantal Welch," she exhaled twice and stepped onto the stage. Embarrassed by the glowing introduction, Chantal tentatively strode to the podium.

Inhaling to calm her nerves, she hoped no one heard her knees banging against the podium. Placing her notes on the shelf, she realized that her hands were shaking too much to even consider taking a sip of water.

With no way to escape, Professor Chantal Welch grabbed the sides of the lectern and searched the crowd for Crystal. Locating her in the third row, she saw her friend surreptitiously holding a pair of black socks. Their eyes locked. Crystal smiled and pointed to her eyes.

Chantal relaxed and began her speech. Half forcing a smile, she spoke quietly, "Ladies and gentlemen, distinguished guests, friends. Sisler University was the first business college to require corporate ethics courses for MBA students. It was a tough fight, but it was worth it. Our business leaders must act responsibly—without exception."

She shifted her gaze to the row behind Crystal and found another friendly face. Chantal's jaws relaxed and she directed her remarks to a man with green eyes. Scouting the crowd, she locked in on one face after another and spoke as if she had but one listener. With each set of friendly or hungry eyes, she gained confidence. Her voice grew stronger and her message filled the auditorium.

The disappointed gators spotted Professor Winston Anderson starting to sweat and made their way from the podium to his side, focusing on a much larger meal.

Chantal Welch, with advice from her friend, faces her fears, plunges ahead, and drives away her gators.

You can do the same thing. Whether it is fear of public speaking, trepidation about calling that certain someone for a date, a sales call, a job interview, meeting with the boss, or talking to your children about drugs.

Remember to address the individual, the human face, and not the crisis.

Face your fear and plunge ahead.

FIFTEEN

Act Brave, You Might Fool the Gators

If animals sense fear, doesn't it follow that they sense the absence of fear, as well?

It helps to project a confident image. Not false bravado, but the quiet confidence of knowing you can solve the problem. If the people around you think you have *an idea* of how to solve the problem, it inspires them to follow you.

You are the leader; lead by example.

> Kristin Peranoski was incensed. For at least the fifth time this year, her boss, Sabrina Abernathy, took credit for work Kristin had done. This time Sabrina passed off the new employee bonus program as her original idea.
>
> Once again, senior management lauded Sabrina for something Kristin or one of her co-workers had originated and developed. The praise never trickled down to anyone in the department. Sabrina alone basked in the spotlight.
>
> Kristin, uncomfortable with confrontation, especially with her boss, did not challenge Sabrina. Sabrina received the praise,

recognition, and bonuses. Kristin worked and stoked a fire of resentment.

Those inner fires did not deter a young female alligator from staking out the space behind Kristin's credenza as a new home.

Kristin is trapped in a situation many people face, held hostage by a paycheck. Because they cannot afford to walk away from their jobs, they accept the abuse.

To avoid creating more problems for themselves, such as losing their jobs, they keep quiet. As the abuse continues, it increases their stress level. Resentment grows and manifests in their attitude at work and their behavior at home.

Counseling is one option, because it can help people learn to deal with the stress and resentment. Individual and group counseling can help people recognize the causes and effects of their stress, and it provides an outlet for blowing off steam.

Kristin, however, chooses another course. She is prepared to stand up to the bully.

Several weeks later Kristin completed another project, an employee satisfaction survey. As she burned the final version of her document onto a CD-ROM, she stared into the eyes of her nephew's picture and remembered a conversation the two of them had recently.

When seven-year-old Alec told his aunt he had been harassed by a bully all year, she advised him to "stand up to the bully or he will keep picking on you." A few days later Alec took her advice and confronted the bully. The bullying ceased.

Kristin spoke to Alec's picture, as well as herself, "Time for me to stand up to the bully." After a few minutes, a smile came to her face. She had a plan.

If it worked, her career at Pitch and Ketch might become more pleasant. If it didn't work, she would have to change employers. That wasn't a big deal, because working for the largest outplacement service east of the Mississippi was not fun.

Don't Tick Off the Gators!

Using Office Scheduler, Kristin scheduled a meeting with Sabrina for nine o'clock the next morning. She sent a blind, information-only notice to three of her research associates and to Sabrina's boss, Daphne Wing.

Next, she burned two additional copies of her CD, with date and time stamps. Placing one in her briefcase, she altered her exit route. Instead of walking directly to her car, she detoured through the research wing and stopped at the corporate library.

Kristin registered her CD with the librarian, and asked for a numbered receipt. Her work was now an officially registered Pitch and Ketch corporate document, recorded with the day's date.

She photocopied the receipt, placed it and another CD into an interoffice envelope, and addressed it to Daphne Wing. She deposited the envelope in the library's outbox on her way out the door. She smiled to herself as she left for the evening. "Tomorrow is going to be a big day," she said aloud.

The young gator sighed and returned to her sleep.

At precisely eight fifty-five the next morning, Kristin walked into Sabrina's office, exchanged the usual morning greetings, and handed her the CD labeled "Employee Satisfaction Survey." Confident in her work, she sat across from her boss, prepared to discuss the merits of the project and its value to Pitch and Ketch.

Sabrina inserted the CD into her PC and reviewed the document. She tried to hide that fact that she was impressed. "This is excellent," she whispered under her breath.

With a practiced polish, she looked at her watch and spoke apologetically, "Kristin I'm sorry, but right before you arrived I received a call. I hate to cut the meeting short, but I'm needed in administration right away. I'll look at this later and let you know what I think."

With a tremble in her throat, Kristin replied, "I understand. Why don't I keep the CD until we can meet again?"

"No need, dear. I'll review it and get back with you later."

"Today?" Kristen squeaked.

"Later. As I said, something came up," Sabrina blurted.

Kristin started to rise and leave, then she thought of Alec and sat back down. Keeping her defiance somewhat in check, she spoke quietly, "It isn't going to work this time, Sabrina."

"What do you mean by that?" Sabrina's voice rose as she took offense to Kristen's tone.

"Just what I said. You are not taking credit for my work anymore," Kristen said, boldly.

Feeling slightly energized, Kristin continued, "You passed the bonus plan off as your own. You have taken all of the credit for a lot of the work done by the people in our department. But not this time."

"You are out of line!" Sabrina roared.

"Maybe. But you can't steal this one from me," Kristen confidently replied.

Slightly taken aback, Sabrina smiled smugly and snapped, "It's your word against mine."

"I thought you would say that." Kristin reached into her briefcase and handed Sabrina a copy of the corporate library receipt.

Sabrina stared at the paper and grew pale.

Kristin, sensing her boss's embarrassment and anger, sat silently and waited for Sabrina to speak.

After an awkward pause, Sabrina gulped and looked up. Slowly she began, "I could fire you for insubordination. I could make your life a living hell and give you every crappy assignment possible. You do realize that, don't you? Coming in here, accusing me of 'stealing' your work. Do you *think* you have a chance in a power struggle, young lady?"

Kristin composed herself, then in a measured voice said, "Sabrina, you and I know the truth. So does everyone in the department. You take the work we do, copy it, and pass it off to Daphne as your own. How will you explain it when several people in the department make the same claim?"

Sabrina stared at Kristin, smiled, and whispered, "Nice trick, registering the CD. Well, I find this work unacceptable. As your superior, I can have the CD deleted from the library."

"Can you delete the copy that Daphne has?"

"What?" Sabrina was clearly stunned.

"I sent Daphne a copy, as well. I don't think she will find it unacceptable."

Sabrina was dumbfounded. That could ruin her. She needed time to recover.

"I think we need to take a break and discuss this later."

"May I have my CD until then?"

Reluctantly, Sabrina closed the program and removed the CD from her computer. Slowly, she handed it back to Kristin. "I hope you will keep this between the two of us. In fact, why don't you take the rest of the day off, and we'll discuss this tomorrow? You know, cooler heads and all that."

"No, thanks. I'll stay here. I have plenty of work to do and want to be ready to discuss this with you after you take care of the issue in administration. Or I can discuss it with Daphne Wing, whoever has the time—first." With that she marched out of the office, closing the door very gently as she exited.

A small group of gators slinked into a corner of Sabrina's office and waited for lunch.

Kristin's actions are bold. Standing up to her boss is one kind of danger; going over the boss's head is definitely the move of a brave (or desperate) person. It is a risky and dangerous ploy, at best—suicidal if it fails. Kristin decides there is nothing to lose, and she gambles.

Daphne Wing wondered why Kristin would send her an information-only email, especially about a meeting with her boss. Her curiosity doubled when she opened the interoffice envelope containing the CD. After reading the document, she was impressed and somewhat perplexed to receive it outside the normal chain of command.

Using the intercom, she instructed her assistant, Edna Cey, to call Kristin and ask her to come to her office.

Moments later, Kristin arrived and was led in.

"Ms. Peranoski, this employee satisfaction survey is an excellent idea. It is well developed and will be useful internally and for our clients, as well," Daphne said sincerely.

"Thank you. I'm glad you liked it," responded Kristin with a smile.

"I am curious. Why did you send it to me?" Daphne asked.

"Mrs. Wing," Kristin swallowed and proceeded, "there has been a problem with work in our department being passed off as that of our boss."

"That is a pretty strong statement. Was any of the work you reference yours?" she said as she sternly eyed Kristen.

"Yes. The bonus plan," Kristen confidently replied.

"This is a very serious charge. Can you prove it?"

"Yes. I keep copies of all my work, originals and revisions," Kristen answered.

Thinking intensely, Daphne faced Kristin and spoke in a very calm and measured tone, "Very well. I will investigate this myself. Naturally, I will discuss the situation with Sabrina Alexander. If your accusations are true, you will receive the appropriate bonuses. If the charges are not true, you will face the consequences, and they could be severe. Do you understand that?"

"Yes, ma'am. I can deliver my copies of the bonus plan to you as soon as I duplicate the CD," Kristen politely answered.

"I see. Please give it to Edna Cey. I must emphasize that I need your discretion in this matter. Can I count on it?" Daphne winked with her question.

"Yes, you can," Kristen assured her.

Kristin left the office feeling exhilarated and a bit apprehensive.

The next afternoon Edna Cey hand-delivered a packet to Kristin.

It contained several items: a note from Daphne Wing, expressing gratitude for her excellent work, diligence, and discretion. It also included an incentive check for the bonus plan and Daphne's bonus recommendation for the employee satisfaction survey. The final item was a handwritten invitation from Daphne to join her for lunch on Friday—to discuss Kristin's career goals.

While Kristin was basking in the glow of justice served,

Sabrina angrily packed her personal belongings. She did this under the watchful eye of the Pitch and Ketch security director.

Neither of them noticed the two gators that climbed into one of the boxes she was packing, the one containing Daphne's management and reference books.

Kristin Peranoski is fed up. She resents Sabrina's actions and feels there is little to lose. So little to lose that she accepts the risks and devises a plan to recover her professional dignity. She feels betrayed and takes the only action she can—she stands up to the bully. Kristin takes a chance and scares off her gators. It worked for her, and it can work for you.

SIXTEEN

Complete Your Plan

You analyze the situation, determine if help is available, seek an appropriate solution, and prime yourself for action. It is time to complete your plan and prepare for action. It is time to get rid of the gators.

Does your plan address the situation honestly and accurately? This is not the time for self-delusion. Be honest. You need to act on reality, not fantasy. Rehearse the plan in your mind, playing out the most likely scenarios. To proceed with confidence, you need to know your plan will succeed more times than it will fail.

Under ideal circumstances, or in a corporate environment, you can debate the merits of your plan, conduct a feasibility survey, and wait for an eighty percent probability of success before acting. However, your situation may not provide the luxury of protracted planning; you need to solve the problem quickly and get out of the swamp.

In a crisis, a sixty-forty success ratio may be enough to proceed. In more extreme situations, with less than a fifty percent likelihood of success, having a well-defined plan may be your best chance to surpass the odds. Many people defeat the gators and escape from the swamp because they believe in their plan. You can do the same.

What has changed since you first realized you were in a predicament? Are there more gators? Are the gators more agitated than when you first encountered them? Or have some of them crawled away?

If the situation has changed, your plan must reflect the current circumstances, not the original crisis. As a leader, you must adapt to reality and attack the problem as it is, not as it was.

Establish the final plan, determine the probability of success, and then act.

> Mason Russell and Gavin Lopes had taken enough abuse from their boss in six weeks to fill three lifetimes. Mason and Gavin are the business development department for Wilde Ideas, a management-consulting firm. Myron Wilde, the owner and founder, gave the adjectives "overbearing and obnoxious" a human face.
>
> Myron's latest ploy was a gem. He has decided to pit Gavin and Mason against each other. He summoned them to his office and announced rather pompously, "Whoever gets the biggest deal this week has a job. The loser is unemployed." Then he turned toward his credenza and began punching numbers for a telephone call, which signalled the end of the conversation and their dismissal.
>
> As the two stunned friends walked back to their office, they did not see a very large, hungry gator stretched out under the conference table they shared.

And you think your boss is a jerk?

Myron Wilde is a pompous, arrogant bully. He is also shortsighted and about to learn the definition of "hoisted by his own petard."

> Mason and Gavin were unable to speak; they just looked at each other, trying to find the words to describe their feelings. For minutes they sat quietly, each trying to determine how they could defeat Myron. Their working relationship had evolved into a solid friendship. Each reveled in the success of the other man, and they often worked as a team to close a deal.

"Gavin, without a doubt, we need to teach that guy a lesson."
"I agree. We don't need any more aggravation from that pompous jerk. Do you have any ideas?" answered Gavin.
"Not yet; how about you?" asked Mason.
"One. Let's get out of here and grab an early lunch," Gavin said with a grin.
"Gavin, it isn't even nine-thirty!" Mason gasped.
"I said early. Besides, what's he going to do, fire us?" Gavin chuckled.

They walked outside into a sunny, muggy morning. What they did not notice was that their new associate, Mr. Gator, had followed them.

A short drive took them to Molly's Hideaway, their favorite restaurant. On their way to an unoccupied booth in the back, they ordered coffee and rolls. For several minutes they chatted about baseball and golf until Mason snapped his fingers and blurted out, "That's it!"

"What?" Gavin said, startled.
"The way to beat Myron," Mason said.
"And that is?" Gavin frowned.
"Simple. Instead of losing one, he loses both of us," Mason announced.
"Okay, there has to be an upside to that plan that I do not see," Gavin said with a groan.
"You will. Finish your coffee and hear me out," Mason said confidently.

Mason lowered his voice, rested his crossed arms on the table, and began explaining the plan. The longer he talked, the more animated he became. He concluded, "Do you think we can pull this one off?"

Gavin smiled and said, "I like it. It just might work."

They exchanged ideas that added substance to the framework Mason provided. What began as an abstract idea now evolved into a very specific and workable plan, which they outlined quickly.

The two men decided to return to the office and start working on their plan on Myron's dime. After leaving several bills on the table to cover the check and tip, they left the restaurant feeling more energized than when they had entered.

On the way to the car, they once again failed to notice a confident Mr. Gator, who still considered them his next big meal, trailing at a discreet distance.

Gavin and Mason used the remainder of the morning to refine the plan. Four well-timed telephone calls resulted in a meeting with the CEOs of the area's largest employers. Working through their normal lunch hour and into the afternoon, they prepared presentation manuals for a breakfast meeting the next day. After checking and rechecking each other's work almost obsessively, they stopped to breathe.

Gavin stood and stretched. "Mason, we have a solid plan, and I believe it will work."

"Yes, it will. I just hope we haven't overlooked anything," replied a brain dead and bone weary Mason.

"If we have not found it by now, we never will. Friend, we have an excellent proposal, four interested clients, and a price they cannot refuse. Most importantly, we developed an opportunity for the six of us to stick it to Myron!"

They locked up and left the building a little after four o'clock.

Mr. Gator trailed them but couldn't decide which to follow home. Slightly annoyed and more than a bit hungry, he slinked into the hedges surrounding the building and waited for his meal to return the next day. Silently, he vowed that they would suffer for making him wait.

Gavin and Mason prepare a plan to get rid of their personal gator. They refine it and are ready to swing into action.

After the four CEOs were seated in a private dining room of the University Club, Mason and Gavin thanked them for coming. Smiling nervously, Mason opened the discussion. "This food looks far too good to let it get cold while I talk."

When the chuckles ended, he continued, "After we eat, Gavin and I would like the four of you to look at a business plan. A plan designed to serve two purposes: one, to provide you with a low cost management consulting program and, two, to establish a new business consortium with the four of you as the founders and charter members." He smiled and sat opposite Gavin.

The four CEOs—Edmund McNally of Valley Medical Center, Camille Palmer of American Bank, Lance Cuellar of Central Communications, and Reed Dobson of Valley Manufacturing—listened politely as Mason spoke.

They chatted amicably while they ate. The easy conversation helped relax the two nervous hosts. As soon as the tables were cleared, Gavin and Mason distributed the proposals to the CEOs.

"For the past three years, Wilde Ideas has not been successful in obtaining your business. Today, we have an idea that will change that," began Mason.

"Quite frankly," interrupted Reed Dobson, "your boss makes it very difficult to *want* to do business with you. How can you change that?"

"Reed, he isn't involved in this plan—just Gavin and me. Please hear us out," Mason assured him.

Reed's left eyebrow shot up in surprise. He nodded for Mason to continue as he leaned forward to listen. The others gave their full attention to Mason as well.

"Last year we designed a management training program named *Management Development College*. The courses are pretty intense: one eight-hour session per quarter.

"Each course is divided into morning and afternoon classes. Everyone, both managers and 'C level' executives, attends a group session in the morning. In the afternoon they are divided into smaller groups, each addressing a particular topic. For discussion purposes, we propose six courses: Supervision, Conflict Management, Human Resource Issues, Professional Writing, Public Speaking, and Career Development."

He looked at his audience and sensed their unspoken approval. Gaining confidence, he went on, "Please turn to page eight of your handout. The first month of each quarter, we will host a 'C Level Conference' for you, your COOs, CFOs, and CIOs.

"The second month is for senior managers and the third for front line managers. A topic for each meeting is already planned; however, we are open to suggestions from you and your managers."

Camille was impressed and spoke first, "This is very interesting. Why haven't we seen this presentation before?"

"Myron didn't like it," Gavin responded flatly.

"Too progressive or not his idea?" cracked Lance.

"Both," Mason and Gavin simultaneously replied.

The entire group laughed out loud.

Mason drew in air, then spoke soberly, "We think this intense training is efficient and effective. Your people are off site for one day a quarter, not for two or three days. It provides each management level with courses designed to help them become more effective leaders. The curriculum can be amended annually, based on your needs and our resources.

"Within six months, we will expand. We want to offer courses for new supervisors, provide a training center, and sponsor seminars. We want to become your management training center. Our goal is to make this the premier management training facility in the state within three to five years.

"We need your financial support and assistance in refining the plan. Will you help us?" Mason held his breath.

"What is the cost?" asked Edmund.

"Edmund, why am I not surprised *you* asked that question first?" interjected a beaming Reed.

Forcing himself to smile, Gavin began his portion of the presentation. "Please turn to page twenty-five. The table presents the start up costs, tuition, and projected revenues.

"With all four organizations attending the same sessions we can offer a lower price. Another big plus is the opportunity for your executives and managers to network and discuss management issues across industries. Think of the opportunity they have to learn from other lines of business!"

After answering a few questions, Gavin stopped to make

sure he had everyone's attention. "Mason and I need to speak off the record."

They took the four CEOs into their confidence and related the previous day's events. Mason concluded by telling them of the numerous times they begged Myron to seriously consider the *Management Development College*.

The four executives exchanged knowing glances, smiled, and shook their heads.

Camille Palmer again broke the silence. "I think we all agree on the premise and need to define the business premise. Am I correct, gentlemen?"

She accepted the nods and smiles from her peers as agreement, so she continued, "What do you need from us, and when do you need it?"

"We need a commitment from you four and your businesses to help us develop this." Swallowing, Gavin added, "Whether Myron agrees or not."

"Let's hope he doesn't," Lance blurted.

"Could you gentlemen excuse us for, say, fifteen minutes?" asked Edmund.

Mason and Gavin left the room, knowing the topic of discussion. After less than thirty minutes, Reed and Edmund found Gavin and Mason pacing in the lobby like two expectant fathers.

"Gentlemen, would you please rejoin us?" asked Edmund.

Without exchanging a word, the four men reentered the meeting.

Camille spoke first. "This is a brilliant plan and we want to provide you the opportunity to develop it. This area needs an economic boost and this could be it.

"My bank will provide the initial financing and the four of us will be your charter clients. There are two conditions, neither of which is negotiable.

"One, the four of us and a few, select companies of our mutual choosing, will form an advisory board to help develop the curriculum.

"Two, this venture does not include Myron Wilde. You gentlemen will be the managing partners. We will provide you with appropriate salaries and work out an equity arrangement. If Myron is involved, the deal is off."

"Can you accept those terms?"

Gavin and Mason looked at each other, smiled broadly and nodded. Gavin's answer was a beat ahead of Mason's, and both said, "Yes!"

Camille returned their smiles and continued, "We'll work out the details of the agreement with your attorney and accountant."

After a brief discussion, the four executives prepared to leave. Lance Cuellar turned to Gavin and Mason and asked, "How do you plan to tell Myron about this?"

They shrugged in unison.

"May I make a suggestion?"

"Please," Mason said.

"Go back to the office and resign effectively immediately. Tell him you decided to go out on your own and start the *Management Development College*. Of course, he'll bust your chops about how it will fail and tell you that you don't have the *cojones* to succeed. Just listen to him and try not to laugh. Then clean out your desks and leave. I'll take care of the rest tomorrow."

Mr. Gator, possessing a keen business sense, decided to head back to Wilde Ideas and locate Myron, who suddenly earned the title "most likely to be eaten."

Our heroes developed the *Management Development College* plan years ago, but Myron, in his finite wisdom, does not want to invest time or money on what he calls "a truly stupid idea."

When Mason and Gavin find themselves surrounded by gators, they modify the plan to reflect their current situation (reality), seek help, and work their way out of the swamp. It isn't luck that lands them the deal; it is preparation and reaching out to others for help.

Mason and Gavin typed their resignations and marched into Myron's office. With some satisfaction, mixed with trepidation, they delivered the news both verbally and in writing.

"You two clowns couldn't *recognize* a business, much less start one. Put together, you two don't have enough brains or guts to run a business. Neither of you has an iota of business sense. Not one shred of business sense.

"As I told you more than once, the idea sucks! I'll bet you anything that you'll be back here begging me for jobs in six months!" bellowed Myron.

"Six, nothing! Two months," he continued. "I'll save you the trip; you are not welcome back here—ever!" Then he launched into a profane recap of their career at Wilde Ideas.

Gavin and Mason sat stoically and listened. When Myron wound down, they returned to their office and packed their personal belongings. Forty-five minutes later, they walked out of Wilde Ideas as free men.

As they passed Myron's office, neither man noticed Mr. Gator crawling in to visit Myron.

The next morning Lance Cuellar pulled his Jaguar alongside Myron, who was preparing to walk his kids into school. "Good morning, Myron."

"Lance, nice ride. When do you have to return it to your Daddy?"

Ignoring the snide remark, Lance asked matter of factly, "Did you know that I'm in a consortium with Camille Palmer and some others to develop the *Management Development College*? We think it is just the shot in the arm local businesses need, enough so to fund it! Gavin and Mason hit a home run with this idea." Smiling broadly, he added, "Have a great day!"

Myron's jaw dropped open like a well-oiled hinge.

Before Myron could respond, Lance rolled up his window and drove away from the school. In his rearview mirror, he saw Myron grimace, turn red, and yell at his kids.

He also thought he saw a rather large gator sink his teeth into Myron's behind.

Myron hoists his own petard; his scheme blows up in his face. He not only drives away two employees, but his bullying creates an opportunity for them to successfully market an idea he had rejected—an idea four other successful business leaders are willing to finance and promote.

Gators love to feast on the proud, especially the fallen proud, more than the weak and defenseless.

SEVENTEEN

Is the Plan Flexible?

You realize that you are still surrounded by gators. Unpredictable, angry, and hungry amphibians that did not receive a copy of your plan and do not know how you expect them to react. Life, too, is unscripted, so you want to make sure your plan allows you to make changes as the situation unfolds. You need flexibility to meet new challenges.

You may need to counter the gators' actions, especially if they do not react as you planned. If they head in a particular direction, the smart move is for you to head in the opposite direction. If they suddenly start climbing the banks, advancing toward you, then running away quickly and leaping onto high ground are good reactions, planned or not.

Trust your instincts. You review the plan and believe you will succeed. You think about how the gators will act and plan accordingly. Make sure you have options if the gators react differently than you expect. It is time to solve the problem and flexibility will help you do it.

Valdora Buckner faced a nearly impossible deadline. Her client, Goeng, Goeng, and Gahn, needed a new management plan by July 3, just three days away. Valdora's normal time frame to develop a management plan was ten days, if everything went smoothly. Unfortunately, Goeng, Goeng, and Gahn wasn't a smooth operation; they need help in a hurry. They need so much help they were willing to pay a premium to receive it quickly.

Goeng, Goeng, and Gahn was a public relations firm owned by two brothers, both former major league baseball players, and their cousin. The three men had college degrees, charisma, contacts, and absolutely zero business sense.

They had somehow survived for five years, eking out a small profit each year. Their accountant advised them to develop a strategic plan, because the company needed direction and fiscal discipline.

Fortunately for Valdora, they shared the same accountant, and he referred them to her. Once she got past the elation of working with a new client, she knew working with the brothers and their cousin was going to be a challenge.

She packed her briefcase with project files and notes and thought she saw three tiny but rather ugly alligators climb into the briefcase. Too much work, she thought, I'm seeing things. She locked the door and stepped into the heavy, muggy afternoon air.

Hours later, after a bike ride and shower, Val stared at her notes. "These guys don't know how to run a business," she thought, half-aloud.

Brock and Aaron Goeng could attract business and make money, that was a given. But she knew they didn't have a grip on expenses and didn't know how to establish a price structure. "What they need is a professional manager," she said to the quiet whir of the air conditioner.

Bradford Gahn, the cousin, was listed as operations manager, but he was not versed in finance. He was a marketer forced to play manager. Val thought, Maybe I could sell them a

Don't Tick Off the Gators! 109

management service; one of my consultants could run the operation. They would have the professional management they need, and I would have a steady revenue stream.

Val triumphantly raced to her computer, pulled up a proposal template, and began filling in the blanks of a standard management services contract. In less than thirty minutes, she was sure she had a new and lucrative client.

One small, ugly gator yawned and wondered when someone would feed him. The other two slept.

Valdora feels pretty good; she develops a quick solution using one of her standard plans. She doesn't realize that she is making an error in using a cookie cutter approach to solve management problems for an unconventional company.

Gators love cookie cutter approaches. They consider them free dessert, and gators love free food, especially desert.

As Val proofread the contract for typos and misspellings, she couldn't shake an uneasy feeling. She felt as if an invisible friend was telling her that this plan just might not be right.

Brock and Aaron were extremely loyal to Bradford. While playing in the majors, they hired him as their personal assistant before he graduated from college. When they started the business, they hired him to run it while they golfed with clients and made personal appearances.

Bradford was loyal to them, as well. He always looked after their best interests, took good care of them, and they could trust him. Suggesting a professional manager to replace Bradford might offend them.

Val was distracted by a loud noise from her television. A has-been actor, shilling for a Medicare supplemental insurance commercial, was enumerating the benefits of some new policy. She thought he looked like her Uncle Malachi.

Uncle Mal retired after a 35-year career working for a local insurance company, the last 25 as controller. His days were filled with golf, gardening, and helping senior citizens solve their medical insurance problems. He enjoyed working with the seniors for two reasons: they needed him and the mental stimulation made him feel worthwhile.

As she thought of Uncle Mal, she whispered, "Too bad he doesn't have more of a challenge."

Like a well-turned double play, the answer came to her in one fluid thought: Uncle Mal could help Bradford, especially with his management skills. Instead of replacing Bradford, the Goengs could hire Uncle Mal to mentor him. Uncle Mal could teach him how to run a business professionally and profitably.

Val jumped up, called Uncle Mal, and gave him a detailed account of the situation. He listened and immediately agreed to consult each week. After six months, they would reassess the situation. Val was relieved, and Mal was excited about the challenge. They thanked each other and ended the call with a promise for lunch and golf on Saturday.

Val sat down and typed a second proposal and prepared for her meeting with the Goengs.

Somewhere in her briefcase a miniature gator realized dinner was not being delivered, so he crawled out and began to look for another source of food. His friends kept sleeping.

On July 2, Val met with Brock, Aaron, and Bradford. They were eager to learn how she could help them and listened to the idea about Malachi Buckner mentoring Bradford. As she finished speaking, the three men exchanged smiles.

Brock lead off, saying, "That is a great idea, Val. I would like to suggest one change. The truth is that all three of us need to learn how to run a business, not just Brad. Will your Uncle Malachi work with all three of us?"

"I'm sure he would be delighted to do that. He loved watching you guys play," Val assured them.

Val follows her gut feeling that the cookie cutter approach will not work. When she creates a custom approach for Goeng, Goeng, and Gahn, she hits a home run.

Her clients will receive the help they need, and she learns the importance of flexibility.

Three gators are denied a meal, although two are still sleeping and don't know what happened.

EIGHTEEN

Make the Plan Work

You can succeed if you execute the plan and are flexible enough to react to any changes. Once you decide fighting the alligators is your only option, do not allow negative thoughts to take control. You must believe that you can and will succeed.

You may need to make changes on the fly. React to the situation, modify your plan as the situation warrants, and work toward your goal. Valdora Buckner ("Make the Plan Flexible") bases her changes on a gut feeling that her standard, cookie cutter approach will not work, and she is right. Her new plan is a winner.

If help is available, accept it. You don't have to fight the battle alone. Val knows she needs a specialist and seeks her Uncle Malachi's help. Follow her example. If you know someone who can help you defeat the gators, ask for their help.

> Caleb Hillerich and Jonas Bradsby couldn't believe the email, even after reading it a third time. They understood the words but could not accept them as truth.

Their breakthrough project, a promotional film for the local Chamber of Commerce, was in jeopardy. Victor Garcia, the voice-over man they had pursued for months, decided to work on another project "that more closely matched his professional skills." Yesterday they thought his involvement was guaranteed.

Caleb was hot when he proclaimed, "He was never serious about working for us. As soon as a better deal came along, he left us like dogs. Even I know that 'more closely matched with my professional skills' means he got more money."

He paced and added, "He wasn't man enough to tell us face-to-face or give us the opportunity to match his offer. No, he sends an email and 'his sincerest regrets.' Sincere is not the 'S word' that comes to mind." A string of angry profanities followed as he let off steam.

Jonas let him vent. He thought for a moment and stroked his chin, "We staked our reputation on this film. We sank all our capital into equipment and production costs. We counted on Victor's voice and reputation to give us credibility. Victor or no Victor, we have a contract and need to complete the project, old buddy. We must finish it, and it must be a success. What do we need to do to achieve that?"

Caleb stared at his friend and partner, amazed at how cool he was. Even now, with a deadline staring them in the face, Jonas acted as if they had weeks, not days, to complete the film.

Caleb thought he saw something slinking along the outer walls of the office. It looked like a pack of alligators. Man, I must be seeing things, he thought.

Jonas smirked. "What we need, old friend, is to have James Earl Jones or James Coburn walk into H & B Productions and ask if we could use free help."

A smile spread across Jonas's face. "On the off chance they don't happen to show up in the next ten minutes, I may have another idea."

"And it is?" Caleb asked.

"Remember that kid, Lyle, who used to sit way up in the

stands at the American Legion Ball Park and pretend he was broadcasting the game? You know, the guy who talked into a portable tape player?"

"Yeah, I heard a couple of those tapes, and he was good. Odd kid, but a good announcer," Caleb said.

"Well, Lyle is a broadcast communications major at Michigan, and he's home for the summer. I'll bet he would help us out."

"How much will he cost us?"

Jonas smiled again. "Less than Victor Garcia. A lot less."

Caleb tried to suppress a grin. "You gonna call him or should I?"

"I will. He used to hang out with my cousin," Jonas said.

Jonas Bradsby thinks, while Caleb Hillerich fumes. After he runs through the available options, Jonas arrives at a plan that will employ the best weapon available, an eager broadcast communications major. Because he is more focused on the problem than his partner, he arrives at a solution.

In times of crisis, focus on the solution.

The next morning, an eager Lyle Martin arrived before seven o'clock to meet with Caleb and Jonas. In fifteen minutes, they agreed on his salary and by seven-twenty he was intently watching the film and making notes on the script.

"I'll be ready to tape the voice-over by nine," Lyle stated confidently. "It's pretty straightforward. We can complete this today, guys. Piece of cake."

The gators raised their heads slightly, looked at each other, and closed their eyes. They were always confident their next dinner would consist of two filmmakers. Now they thought they might also get a side dish of "talking head."

Minutes before they began taping, Lyle asked if he could amend the script. "For example, when we show Memorial Field and Veterans Park, we could add 'We remember those who sacrificed for us.' What do you think?"

Jonas and Caleb did not hesitate; they enthusiastically nodded their consent. It was time to begin taping.

Lyle's talent and burgeoning professionalism was readily apparent; he became one with the movie. His deep, sonorous voice, inflections, local flavor, and exquisite timing were the touch the film needed.

They called it a wrap at four o'clock. Jonas and Caleb had every reason to feel confident about the project. Their film and Lyle's voice had the look and sound of a winner.

Jonas, Caleb, and their film editor worked all night; they completed the final version closer to dawn than midnight. Afterward, they toasted their impending achievement with bottled water, and promised that it would be champagne after a successful premiere.

Both men wearily trudged home for showers and a nap. They agreed to meet at nine o'clock to prepare for the grand premiere that was scheduled for noon.

The gators were agitated. No dinner, no snack, and some very happy movie makers. They began to wonder if their own starvation was imminent.

As the Chamber members watched their film, Jonas and Caleb paced in the back of the room. Their confidence sagged. They couldn't see any faces and could not judge the crowd's reaction.

When the theme song played for the last time and the credits began to scroll down the screen, the crowd burst into applause, some standing. When the lights returned to normal, the two filmmakers walked toward the crowd. By now, almost everyone was standing and applauding. Jonas and Caleb had succeeded!

They heard a multitude of compliments as they walked to the podium. They beamed and their chests swelled as they stood before the hometown crowd.

Jonas spoke first, "Am I correct in assuming that you liked it?"

When the laughter and applause subsided, Caleb leaned into the microphone and asked, "Wasn't Lyle Martin excellent?"

> More shouts of approval and clapping came from the local business leaders.
> As they concluded their remarks, the two men left the podium to another thunderous ovation.
> The young men worked the crowd and accepted the congratulations of the business people who stopped to shake their hands. A few handed Jonas and Caleb their business cards, and inquired about hiring them for promotional videos.
> Jonas and Caleb's years of hard work were about to pay off.
> Several disappointed and hungry-looking gators were seen scrounging for meals on the outskirts of town.

Caleb Hillerich and Jonas Bradsby solve their problem by using an available resource—Lyle Martin. They succeed because they work hard and complete the project—persevering past a major disappointment.

Losing Victor Garcia might stop some people, but not this pair. They make their plan work by trusting their talent and Lyle's voice. It pays off handsomely for all three men.

The gators leave hungry because the combination of Hillerich and Bradsby hit a home run.

NINETEEN

Get Out of the Swamp

You want to not only escape the swamp, you want to do it without losing limbs or a large chunk of hindquarter. The goal is to get away from the gators, not to further antagonize them. It is time to put your well-developed, flexible plan into action.

Make sure your initial steps are in the proper direction—away from the gators. If there are obstacles in your path, remove them, go over them, or go around them. Watch where you plant your feet and take advantage of whatever tools are available. Branches, logs, and rocks are not as deadly as angry gators.

But there is a big difference between lost blood and blood loss. Lost blood is a cut, scrape, or small wound. Blood loss is serious, sometimes fatal. Keep lost blood to a minimum and prevent blood loss—your own or that of your helpers. Lead and protect.

Erica Mantle sat in the spacious and airy lobby of On Deck Personnel Agency, reviewing her presentation. As she did, she tried to gauge the prevailing attitude of employees walking through the lobby. She had a pretty good idea of how most people felt, and she wanted to validate her feeling.

It was the Friday before a three-day weekend and most people are ready to leave. This group was no exception. She sensed that their minds were far away; some of them were already on holiday—mentally. Erica's tension grew as she watched people prepare for the long weekend.

By luck of the draw, she was the fourth and final vendor to meet with On Deck today. She was scheduled to present an employee scheduling-and-tracking software system to the management team. Sales presentations were nerve-wracking enough, without an unspoken "hurry up" from every attendee.

Three young and hungry female gators quietly surrounded Erica. They were impressed with her outfit and decided to spare the lovely Yves Saint Laurent suit when they consumed her.

On Deck, a national temporary employment agency, was known as "one tough customer". Last fall, they fired their advertising agency for misspelling "discreet" in a newspaper advertisement. Two years ago they ended a ten-year relationship with an office supply company because the letterhead was not perfectly centered. In the eyes of Marshall Scully, the founder and CEO, that was unacceptable.

Erica was allotted ninety minutes for her presentation, a hands-on demonstration, and the requisite question-and-answer session. Her mind was a hodgepodge of negative thoughts: They will try to rush me so they can get out of here for the weekend. They'll try to intimidate me into making mistakes. I'm wasting my time; I'll bet they've already selected another vendor.

As Erica's stomach churned, the gators decided they liked her shoes and bag, as well. Soon they began arguing among themselves over who would get which items.

Erica closed her folio and leaned back. She shut her eyes and breathed deeply, cleansing her lungs and clearing her mind. Waves of relaxation rolled in and out with each breath.

Slowly, a profound thought began to center in her mind's eye. Erica sat bolt upright as the thought became clearer. With an eerie calmness, she understood the need to change her approach. Moving to a table in a quiet corner, she booted her laptop and quickly modified the presentation.

Erica realizes that she is walking into a swamp full of gators. People who do not want to sit through a sales presentation can be ruthless and easily agitated. Their impatience can act like a virus; one infected person can spread it rapidly. But Erica has a plan to avoid that potential hazard and get safely out of the swamp.

Minutes after Erica completed the changes, an administrative assistant arrived and escorted her into the conference room. As she placed her handouts on the table, the assistant returned with the bottled water Erica had requested.

Once she was certain that Erica could operate the projector, the assistant wished her good luck and left Erica alone.

The three gators did not enter the conference room; they remained in the lobby, battling over Erica's clothes.

Marshall Scully and eight managers arrived three minutes before the scheduled time and took their seats, scarcely exchanging a word or glance with Erica. Marshall looked at his watch, and when he saw it was straight up two o'clock, he nodded for Erica to begin.

Sensing this group might be impatient, she introduced herself as she walked toward the projector. When she depressed the mouse key, the blue screen showed a single, golden line:

ROI: Give me 20 and I'll give you 70

She spoke with forced confidence, "Ladies and gentlemen, you give me twenty minutes of undivided attention, and I will give you the other seventy minutes. With Mr. Scully's blessing, you can start your holiday weekend early."

Marshall smiled and thundered, "They can follow me out the door!"

After the laughter died down, she continued her presentation, "I'm serious. I need only twenty minutes of your time."

She placed both hands on the table and leaned forward in a friendly yet professional manner. She spoke slowly, saying, "The other vendors told you about their products. They told you how robust, how scalable and how state-of-the-art they were. Each bragged how his or her product was 'exactly what you need.' Am I correct?"

Murmurs of agreement rose from nodding heads.

"They also told you it would take months to install and that you may need to buy new hardware. Somewhere in the presentation they added that they were the nation's oldest, largest, or best known supplier of human resources software."

Hector Pinella, the IT Manager, said, "That pretty much sums up the three other presentations. Of course, it took them five hours to tell us that!"

Laughing with them, Erica smiled. Looking from Hector to Marshall and, finally, to a woman on his immediate right, Erica posed a question, "Did any of them ask you about the intricacies of temporary employees and multiple clients?"

"No," said Samantha Ryan. "They were too busy talking."

Erica looked directly at Samantha and asked, "Do you think that is a problem?"

"Yes, it is. How can they install software for us if they don't know what we need?"

Erica allowed that question to sink in as she clicked the mouse again to change the screen. The words changed to:

Tell me what you need

The people in the room stared at the screen but did not speak. Slowly, everyone looked at Marshall, who was eyeing Erica with great interest.

"Young lady, no one has ever asked us that question. It will take us hours to answer it." He looked around the table and added, "Tell us about your product. We'll save our answers to your question—for now."

"Thank you," Erica said.

She changed the screen:

BEST Tracking

"BEST tracking. Designed for your company, based on your needs," Erica told the group. "It works on most platforms, including your MicroSystem. It doesn't require expensive upgrades, users need only about two hours of training, and it can be fully functional in thirty days."

She clicked the mouse one last time, and the screen read:

Bills automatically

Easy to use and install

Scalable

Tailored for your specific needs

Erica stood in front of her laptop and said, "If you would gather around me, I'd like to walk you through a demonstration of BEST Tracking."

Ten minutes later—nineteen minutes after she first spoke—Erica said, "Ladies and gentlemen, that concludes my presentation. Are there any questions?"

The managers turned to Marshall, who was checking his Rolex.

"Ms. Mantle, you kept your word and gave us an extremely professional presentation. Succinct and factual. Most importantly, you asked the appropriate question, which none of your competitors bothered to ask, 'What do *you* need?'

"You also demonstrated an understanding of our personal needs by graciously shortening your presentation. It has been a long week, and the gift of time is something we all appreciate."

"Thank you, Mr. Scully. I am still interested in finding out what On Deck needs."

"Ms. Mantle, my secretary will call you Tuesday to schedule that meeting. As for the rest you, Ms. Mantle has dismissed us for the weekend, so let's go!"

> The managers thanked Erica for her consideration and raced back to their offices to escape before Marshall could change his mind about leaving early.
>
> Somewhere in the lobby, three teenage, female alligators were still wrestling. As they did, their intended victim walked triumphantly out the door to a wonderful, long weekend. She planned to celebrate her achievement.

Getting out of the swamp requires a first step that avoids the gators. Erica does just that; she seizes the group's attention with her opening statement. And she keeps it.

Erica Mantle succeeds because she is flexible and aware of the circumstances, especially her audience's desire to leave early for a holiday weekend. Her ability to deliver a sales pitch and allow them to start their weekend early is as brilliant as the time McGyver stopped the leak in a Jeep's radiator with a dozen eggs.

Both Erica's and McGyver's plans are inspired and brilliant. More importantly, both plans work.

TWENTY

Relax, You've Earned It

You are a winner. You defeat the gators. Hail to the victor! You escape an alligator infested swamp and complete your mission. What do you do next? The Most Valuable Player of the World Series or Super Bowl gets to answer that question with, "I'm going to Disney World!"

But if you live in the real world and a free trip to Orlando is not on the horizon, what will you do to celebrate *your* hard-fought victory?

First, thank the people who helped you. Express your gratitude to anyone who provided assistance, no matter how seemingly unimportant. Whether they help distract gators or jump into the swamp to help you or rescue you by boat, you owe them *expressed* gratitude.

It is essential that you take time to recover—both mentally and physically. The instant the adrenalin wears off, you will be hungry, thirsty, and exhausted. Rest is the pause that refreshes your mind, body, and spirit.

In the best circumstances, you will have the opportunity to travel to an exotic location for a well-deserved vacation. At a minimum, you need to sleep and reenergize yourself.

As you cleanse your wounds and ice the ego bruises, evaluate the actual losses versus the perceived losses. Examine your scars. Are they permanent or temporary? Are they visible or too small to worry about? Are they new badges of honor? Can you still sit comfortably?

Despite the victory, there may be emotional trauma and scarring. For some, the recent crisis might be the toughest situation they ever faced. That can be overwhelming. Even if you win, you may need medical attention. If the damage is more emotional than physical, you need another type of help. After surviving and winning, there is no shame in needing help of any sort.

You may need to talk with someone to help you deal with the aftermath of your ordeal. It may be a friend, a priest, a coworker, or a professional. If you need counseling to aid your recovery, seek and accept it as part of the healing process. Getting rid of emotional baggage now may help you deal with future gators more easily.

> Gaston Feller felt as if he were climbing a moving mountain. His boss, Randolph Snider, couldn't decide on the physical layout of the new office and was making changes on an hourly basis—so it seemed. Sometime after eight o'clock Saturday evening, Randolph was satisfied with the plan.
>
> Gaston suppressed the urge to tell Randolph that he had rejected the same plan earlier in the week. He knew it was useless and didn't want to delay his escape from Randolph. It was better to remain silent and leave than to start him thinking about more changes.
>
> Gaston sealed the signed plans in a large security envelope and left before Randolph asked to "look at the plans just one more time." As he drove to the office of their architects, Musial and Wagner, he began to wind down and relax. For the first time in weeks, he actually smiled.
>
> His goal was simple: drop the plans into the architect's night delivery box before Randolph could change his mind again. Once he accomplished that, the evening was his, and he planned to enjoy a quiet evening—alone.
>
> Gaston made sure the envelope fell into the secure area of the drop box then drove home on autopilot. His brain was no

longer processing changes and architectural drawings; instead, it turned to thoughts of sitting in his recliner watching a baseball game, while enjoying popcorn and ice-cold beer. He was too exhausted to get out of the car and sat in the darkened garage for several minutes after the light flicked off. Seconds after he entered the house and closed the door, his pager buzzed. Gaston glared at the familiar number, followed by "911"—it was Randolph, indicating this was an "emergency call."

He gritted his teeth as he muttered, "What now?" He sighed and dialed the number.

As he did, a large, angry alligator crawled unnoticed beneath his dining room table.

Like too many executives, Gaston Feller is overworked and under appreciated. He needs to recharge his batteries and clear his mind. He also needs to get rid of a very large and aggravating gator—his ultra-controlling boss.

Randolph, blunt as usual, skipped the pleasantries and launched into his newest concern—their latest crisis. "Will the deal with Stengel Industries pan out? I mean, they're pretty demanding in the negotiations. They want a lot for what they're willing to pay. Are they in a cash crunch?"

Gaston steeled himself for another lengthy conversation with his boss. Randolph was as self-absorbed as he was intruding, which made their conversations one-sided. Randolph never thought to ask if he was intruding or interrupting.

"Randolph, it has been a long week—no, make that a long month. It is past nine o'clock on Saturday night, and I am just too tired to discuss this right now. Stengel isn't going to do anything before Monday morning and, frankly, neither are we. Can we discuss it Monday, when we're both mentally fresh?"

"What is your problem? Our company is on the verge of losing a major deal, and you're *tired*? Maybe I need to find someone else to be my COO. Someone who doesn't tire so easily. Someone with dedication," Randolph sniped at him.

"Randolph, this can wait until Monday. Stengel is on vacation for another week, and nothing is going to happen until he returns and gets involved in the negotiations," Gaston said.

"We need to be prepared for the worst. Let's meet tomorrow in the office at two o'clock. Unless that interferes with your nap," Randolph continued sniping.

Cringing at that last remark, Gaston muttered a terse, "Okay." He regretted the word as soon as it came out.

"That's my *boy*. See you tomorrow." Randolph hung up.

Gaston is at a personal crossroads. He is physically drained, mentally wiped out, and cannot resolve the latest problem tonight. In his heart, he knows that he needs to confront Randolph. He knows he needs to do that soon. He becomes angrier when he realizes how much Randolph controls his life through games and manipulations. He wants to reclaim his life.

Unfortunately, people invite gators into their lives by giving up control of their lives for a job or large salary. Take control of your life and get rid of the gators.

Gaston Feller tossed and thrashed but never fell into a deep sleep. Staring at the wall, then the ceiling and, finally, at the alarm clock, he realized something had to change. He thought, Randolph is always taking and rarely giving. He makes no effort to understand other people or consider their needs, let alone their lives. He loves to control and manipulate.

Gaston knew he had to sleep. He called upon an old relaxation technique and began to release the tension in each muscle, one by one, gradually willing his body to relax. When he allowed his mind to empty, he fell into a deep, restful sleep.

Sunday morning after a bike ride, church service, and a good meal with friends, Gaston felt rejuvenated.

Grudgingly, he began to prepare for his meeting with Randolph. Today, Gaston decided, the agenda will include more than Randolph's insecurities about Stengel Industries; it will include Gaston's concerns about himself.

Don't Tick Off the Gators! 129

Gaston sat on his deck overlooking the bay and reviewed his situation. He was COO in name only. Randolph Snider immersed himself in every decision at Snider Consulting. Randolph had built a successful management consulting firm by driving his employees past their limits. His micro-managing created a ridiculous turnover rate—nearly seventy-five percent per year. The constant change of employees did not please the clients; many had not renewed their contracts with Snider.

Gaston was financially secure. With money in the bank, prudent investments, and enough contacts to land an executive-level position in a number of corporations, he could walk away without any fears. He knew Randolph would liberally throw more money in his direction as an incentive to remain the COO.

Twice he had tendered his resignation, only to have Randolph offer him more money and promise to allow him more managerial control. The money came, but the promises went unfulfilled. Now his dedication and energy were being questioned. "What was next? My intelligence?" Gaston wondered. He decided that today was the day to end his working relationship with Randolph Snider.

Gaston arrived just before two o'clock, unaware that four steps behind him was a slightly peeved gator. As he walked toward Randolph's office, he noticed it was empty. Thirty minutes passed and Randolph had not arrived.

Concerned, as well as angry, Gaston called Randolph's cell phone and asked if he had been delayed by traffic or had changed the meeting location.

"No. I decided to go to the beach this morning. We'll talk tomorrow at seven, over breakfast."

Gaston clicked off the call and said aloud to no one, except an angry gator, "No, we won't."

By four o'clock, the contents of his office were loaded into his car. He drove away from Snider Consulting for the last time as an employee.

The confused and hungry gator was hidden in the trunk of the car. An intelligent amphibian, he decided to learn more about strategic planning and began to read a thick book.

Monday morning, Gaston was awakened by the telephone's ring. He glanced at the clock, noticed it was just past seven, and started to panic. Then he remembered:

I don't have to go in today or ever again.

"Where are you?" Randolph demanded.

"Home." He replaced the receiver and turned off the ringer.

A few minutes after ten, Gaston Feller, dressed in shorts and a golf shirt, walked into Randolph's office and handed him a typed document.

A snarling Randolph barked. "What is this? And where have you been? It is almost lunchtime and you come waltzing in here with a note!"

"I'll save you the trouble of reading it. I resign. Working for you isn't worth the money, the aggravation, or the time. Find yourself another COO!"

"You'll regret this!"

"No, I won't, but you might." Gaston turned and walked out, ignoring the vulgar invective spewed by an angry and reddening Randolph Snider.

An agitated gator crept toward Randolph. He drooled when he sensed a frosted ego and took a large bite of CEO leg.

Gaston Feller stands up to the gator and reclaims control of his life. He realizes that money is not worth the aggravation of working for a control freak.

The good guy wins, and the gator lunches on the bad guy.

TWENTY-ONE

Solve the Problems

You escape the gators, preserving life, limbs, and behind. To complete the mission you must solve the problem(s) that placed you in the swamp. Analyze the problem(s), the causes, and your reactions. Ask yourself several questions and answer them honestly.

- Did I cause the problem?
- Did I create an environment that allowed it to flourish?
- What was the cause of the crisis?
- How did I respond to each event or stage?
- Can this situation be prevented in the future?
- What can I learn from this experience?

Your answers may reveal more than the root cause of the problem; they may reveal elements of your character. If you create the problem or make it worse by not reacting properly, be man or woman enough to accept the blame.

If someone else is at fault, be merciful and gracious, because you may need mercy and grace one day. The crisis may be unavoidable, regardless of who is at fault. Accept the fact that blame cannot always be assigned—sometimes stuff just happens.

Your goal is to identify the origin of the problem and try to prevent a reoccurrence. This may require time, thought, and assistance from others; but if you save a friend, co-worker, or loved one from the swamp, it is worth the effort.

> Travis Spalding could not believe the last four hours. His assistant manager, administrative assistant, and head cashier had resigned. How could that have happened?
>
> It seemed to have been choreographed. In one-hour intervals, they walked in and handed him their resignations with minimal explanation or conversation. The common threads were "I found a new job" and "I'll work out my two weeks notice."
>
> The three employees knew it would hurt Travis. He couldn't replace them quickly; it would take weeks to find people with their skills and experience. After he hired replacements, it would take several more weeks to train them.
>
> In the past six weeks, five employees had resigned or transferred to another department. In Travis's mind, it had to be a conspiracy to make him look bad—nothing else was possible.
>
> Alone in his office and cursing the world for causing him grief, Travis did not notice a family of six alligators making themselves very comfortable under his desk.

Travis Spalding is deep in the swamp. Because he reacts first and thinks second, he exacerbates problems. If he doesn't react properly, he may dig in deeper rather than dig out.

Travis's career is on the fast track. He zoomed through the management training program and frontline management ranks at a record pace, always exceeding his goals and achieving stellar results. Nine months ago, he was promoted to Operations Manager for Coax and Coach, a major financial clearinghouse.

His knowledge and tireless work ethic are legendary at Coax and

Don't Tick Off the Gators! 133

Coach. That, coupled with glowing evaluations, make him the youngest operations manager in the company's long and distinguished history. Travis isn't a social person with very few friends—almost none at work. His biggest fault is his brusque and abrupt manner with people. His mentors and management executives pass this off as "youthful enthusiasm." However, his employees either feel abused or are so offended that they look for an opportunity to get away from him.

Today he has the chance to face the truth about himself and to get rid of his gators.

> Miles Gehrig, executive vice president, overheard a conversation about Travis's bad day and decided to visit the young manager. He started walking down the hall but returned to his office and grabbed a dog-eared paperback. Smiling wryly, he resumed his trip to Travis's office.
>
> Miles waited unnoticed in the doorway and observed Travis reviewing the daily transaction reports. He knocked and politely asked if he could visit for a while.
>
> "Certainly, Mr. Gehrig. What can I do for you?"
>
> Miles closed the door and sat in a wing chair. He didn't speak right away,. When he did, he chose his words carefully. "I understand that you've had an interesting day. Maybe I can do something for you."
>
> "Interesting is an understatement. Three key people resigned today. Five have left this department since I became manager. I guess they don't want to work, or maybe they don't want to work as hard as I need them to work."
>
> "Is that so?" Miles responded.
>
> Taken aback, Travis replied, "I admit I demand a lot. But I am always the first one here in the morning and the last one to leave. *Every* day. You didn't see anyone out there when you came in, did you?"
>
> "No. You are the only one here," Miles admitted.
>
> "Five-thirty arrives and it is like a fire drill around here. No dedication," He looked at Miles and spoke in an apologetic tone, "Sorry, I'm just venting. I do have a plan—I'll hire a temp to fill in as administrative assistant. It will be easy to

replace the cashier from within the company; there are plenty of people who would get substantial raises to do that job. I can do the assistant's job myself until I find a suitable candidate. It will be tough, but I'll manage."

Miles leaned back, smiled, and spoke quietly, "That sounds like a plan to me. But tell me something, how much more turnover can you absorb and still reach your goals? The training alone can slow down processing by a week or two."

"I'll work evenings and weekends to keep it current. Miles, you know I am not afraid of work, and I always exceed my goals," Travis almost whined.

"That you do." Miles looked at the paperback for a moment. "I pray you don't burn yourself out. You have been a rising star since day one; this would be an inopportune time to crash"

Without letting the words sink in, Travis blurted a response. "No, sir, I'm going to get through this. Once I find some people who are willing to work as hard as I do, this department will be the pride of Coax and Coach!"

"I don't doubt you will get there. What if I could help you reach that goal faster?"

"Tell me how, please," Travis almost begged.

"Mind if I tell you a story first?" Miles asked.

Travis leaned forward, elbows on knees and chin resting on his knuckles, like an eager child.

"When I first started in banking, I was as driven as you are—maybe more so. I worked a minimum of ten hours per day and studied banking all weekend. I was going to be promoted to branch manager faster than anyone at FNB. And I was.

"In three months, I lost half my employees. The other half were looking for jobs but hadn't found them yet. Everyone who worked for me was miserable. They were afraid of making a mistake, because they knew that I would be all over them. They didn't do any extra work and rarely spoke to me. You cannot image how tense it was for them and for me."

He chuckled, recalling as he went on, "Naturally, I didn't really care how they felt about me. I was too focused on becoming a vice president. If they thought I was too tough, they could go work elsewhere. Plenty of people needed jobs and were willing to work. If the new people didn't work out, they could be replaced, too.

"One day Nelson Fielding, the managing director, visited my branch. When he treated me to lunch, I was sure it was to promote me.

"He told me that my branch's results were excellent in every measurable area: total assets, new accounts, accuracy, customer satisfaction, and growth. I was ready for the good news and rehearsed my 'acceptance speech.'

"Then his face tightened and he became serious, almost grim. He told me that the executive committee considered me for a new position as a vice president in commercial lending. His next words struck me like a bat to the chin.

"They were concerned about my track record *with people* and promoted someone else. Because I had the highest employee turnover rate in the company, they were 'worried about my management style.' Former employees used words like 'abrupt', 'inconsiderate', and 'impossible to work' for to describe me.

"I was stunned and humiliated. How could this happen to me?"

Travis sat with his mouth open. He finally broke the silence, speaking in sharp bursts. "What? You? I can't imagine you like that. You are so polite and courteous to everyone."

Miles smiled. "Thank you, but I have not always been that way, especially not back then. I just sat there dazed and hurt. I tried to explain it away, but Nelson waved his hand and asked me to listen for five minutes before I said anything else.

"He was brutal. He told me in very direct, blunt words that I needed to change immediately or there would be no future for me at FNB. He said he would not tolerate abusive managers and that I was beginning to fall into that category.

"Then he said something I will never forget. 'Miles, I can offer you a way to fix the problem. If you are willing to work at it.'

"I was relieved and humbled. I swallowed my pride and managed to whisper, 'Mr. Fielding, I will do whatever you ask. Please give me a chance to prove I can change.'

"He smiled and looked straight into my eyes. After a long wait, he said, 'Fine, I'll do that. But I want you to do two things. You need to read one book and call me every Monday at ten o'clock to tell me what you have learned.'

"I stared at him like he had three heads. 'That's all?' I asked.

"'You must apply what you learn,' he said. 'If you do that, the rest will fall into place.'

"'What's the book?' I asked him.

"He smiled slyly and handed me a brand new paperback copy of *How To Win Friends And Influence People* by Dale Carnegie. 'It helped me when I started managing,' he said.

"I looked at Nelson Fielding the way you just looked at me and asked, 'What kind of problems did you have?'

"He grinned. 'I was much worse than you. People called me Lord Nelson to my face and Führer Fielding behind my back.'"

Miles fixed his gaze on Travis and handed him his dog-eared copy of the Dale Carnegie book. "This, my young friend, is for you. As Nelson said, 'I was worse than you.'

"This book turned me and my career around, just as it did for Nelson Fielding. I think it will do the same for you. Men like the three of us are often so driven to accomplish our goals that we neglect the one skill that will help us most, motivating people. We're actually our own worst enemies."

Travis stared at the well-read book, looked away, then at Miles. "How bad am I?"

"Like all young managers, you have talent, but need to learn how to manage people, as well as processes. Your people don't want to work for you any more than mine did for me. This book will help recognize the reasons and correct them. It is that simple," Miles reassured him.

"I'll make you a deal," Miles continued. "You read the Carnegie book and every Tuesday morning we'll meet for breakfast to discuss the concepts and the art of managing people. All I need from you is a commitment to improve."

"I will. Thank you," Travis said humbly.

"Nelson helped me, I will help you, and one day you can help another young man or young woman facing the same problems."

Miles stood up and offered his hand to Travis. Grasping the young manager's hand firmly, he spoke softly and sincerely, "Travis, this is just a bump in the road. Use it as a learning opportunity."

"Yes, sir," Travis sincerely replied.

Miles walked to the door and turned to face Travis. "You'll find some key passages underlined and some margin notes. I've read that book at least two dozen times, and I learned something new with each reading."

"When do you want it back?" Travis asked.

"If I need it, I know where it is," Miles answered.

Travis sat alone for several minutes, reading underlined passages on the well-worn pages.

As he did, the family of gators realized that if they wanted fresh meat, they needed to move on. This human didn't seem like such easy prey after all.

Travis Spalding reads *How To Win Friends And Influence People*, meets with Miles Gehrig for breakfast every week, and learns to manage people, as well as processes.

He faces the need to change and accepts help willingly and graciously. He solves his management problem by learning how to work with people—applying what he learns. In doing so, he gets rid of the gators.

TWENTY-TWO

Start Again, a Bit Wiser

If you want to succeed in your chosen career or life, in general, you must expect an occasional gator assault. It is the gator's nature to lurk in the background, poised to attack. Their mission is to wreak havoc upon your life. If you want to win, you must expect and respond to surprise attacks.

You will have better success against the gators if you are calm and flexible in both thought and action. To think clearly and logically, you must control your emotions. When you think clearly, you see what is happening around you and it provides you the opportunity to react properly.

Rational thought is one trait that makes humans superior to animals. In a gator attack or other crisis, use your mind, as well as your muscles, to subdue the adversary. When emotions override logical thought processes, people end up as gator cuisine.

You must recognize the need for flexibility. When you are surrounded by gators, flexibility is an asset and can help you escape the swamp. Every good plan includes escape routes. You need a plan that is flexible and allows for unexpected reactions by the gators. Unless the terrain is perfectly flat for miles, anticipate bumps, valleys, trees, and other obstacles in your escape route.

If the gators chase you back into the swamp, prove to yourself (and the world) that you are resilient. A swamp teeming with gators is no place for the timid, fearful, or frightened. The meek may inherit the earth, but the resilient will accomplish much more prior to the end of the world.

Defeating the gators can change your outlook. It can transform you into a more vigilant, more attentive, and more flexible person. Once you experience the adrenalin rush of escaping a swamp filled with gators, day-to-day problems will not seem as vexing. Encountering one gator will not create the same fear as before. Because you survived a crisis, you now possess a higher level of inner strength and confidence. You are a tested leader with a war story to tell.

> Casey Ruth replaced the telephone in its cradle and, for the first time in nearly an hour, fully exhaled. He was indebted to Brandi Cobb. At the last minute she extracted him from the jaws of a gator. Casey was grateful that his poor judgment did not cost his company a major client. Or him his job.
>
> He sat with his feet on his desk and replayed the last few days in his mind. It was not pretty, but he needed to relive them.
>
> Casey, a research manager for the acquisition management firm of Mays and McCovey, did not complete a due diligence report on time. His failure nearly caused a multimillion dollar deal with Ripken and Murray to dissolve.
>
> Ms. Cobb, a vice president and his boss, completed the report during her flight to the west coast. Working late into the evening, she salvaged the deal with a series of calls to the two principals, their attorneys, and three sets of accountants. By midnight, faxed agreements were signed and the deal was complete.
>
> Brandi fought the urge to telephone Casey at home and wake him with the good news; instead, she waited until the next morning and called him prior to boarding her flight home.
>
> She informed Casey that she scrambled to cover his professional lapse and rescued the deal. Then she told him to meet her at eight the next morning. "We need to discuss the

importance of completing work on time and keeping me apprised of your progress. Or lack thereof."

Casey Ruth makes several errors. The most conspicuous is not informing his boss when he encounters a problem, one that jeopardizes the deal. He wastes time on trivial aspects of the report, and he ignores issues that are more important. Ultimately, his neglect forces Brandi to rewrite the report and scramble at the eleventh hour to salvage the deal. It isn't a Triple Crown of achievements that he wants in his boss's memory.

Brandi's call creates a mental shift from dread to relief, a change that clouds his thinking. Casey is relieved and thinks all is well. He is oblivious to reality and to a parade of alligators marching into his office, waiting for the opportunity to grab some dead meat.

The next morning Brandi arrived at seven-fifty and summoned Casey for their meeting.

Casey nearly ran to her office and was soon seated at a small conference table. He was intimidated and uncomfortable as Brandi stared at him. Her first remark did nothing to lessen his stress. "Delegating work *up* the corporate ladder is not a wise career move. Wouldn't you agree?"

"Yes, ma'am." Casey squirmed noticeably, hesitant to maintain eye contact.

"Do you know what is most disturbing about the entire situation?"

Casey replied in a quiet, questioning voice, "The report wasn't finished and you had to complete it?"

"That was displeasing, but it's not what I'm after. What else?"

"Because of the stress it put you under?"

"Forget about me. What did you not do?"

They sat in silence as Casey struggled for an answer. Uncomfortable with the silence, he blurted another question, "I didn't ask for help when I realized there was a problem?"

Brandi nodded. She sensed it was time to change her approach and softened her gaze and tone. "Casey, we did not lose the deal. The client was not affected by your errors, and the financial terms did not change. For that we can be grateful. In fact, only three or four people are aware of what *almost* happened.

"What we need to accomplish today is to develop an understanding that will prevent this kind of disconnection and wasted time in the future. Your time was wasted as much as mine. I do not appreciate you or anyone wasting my time, and I do not appreciate you wasting this department's time.

"I want that point understood. Do not waste my time like that ever again. By my time I mean both my personal time and the time I pay you for productive work."

Casey nodded, afraid his voice would crack if he spoke.

Sensing her employee needed to compose himself, Brandi reached for a stack of papers and pretended to read them for a minute. She handed Casey a copy of his report. "You invested way too much time on unimportant items. For example, three pages were devoted to the computer conversion. It warranted two or three *paragraphs,* at most.

"You also included entirely too much detail on data storage and capacity issues. That level of detail is for the technical staff, not for executives who are negotiating a merger of two multinational corporations.

"And for some reason, you felt that the choice of the advertising agency was worth five pages."

Casey wiped his forehead.

"You failed to include the shareholder objections and their threatened lawsuit. Can you explain why? Didn't you think *that* was important?"

Casey looked away, then toward the table. "I lost several pages of notes and I spent a lot of time looking for them. I was embarrassed and panicked. Then I tried to complete the report from memory. I know now that I should have told you that when it happened."

Brandi absorbed Casey's stunning admission before speaking. "Casey, all you had to do was ask Gabriella for a copy of my notes. It would have saved us both a lot of time. What did you lose and when did you lose it?"

"I'm not sure when. Part of my file is missing, mostly the notes from June and July. I looked everywhere. Through my other files, at home, my briefcase, my car, and the recycling bin. I don't know how it happened."

"Casey, losing the notes is a correctable error. Notes can be replaced or duplicated by others who attended the same meetings. We've all lost notes or documents at one time or another."

The anger returned, and she let it flow. "What disturbs me is the way you reacted. You didn't ask for help, and you failed to inform me of the problem. You compounded that by placing this company in jeopardy of losing its credibility and the deal by trying to pass off some horse manure report to a major client.

"I was appalled at some of the verbiage in that report. Our credibility as a company was at risk because you tried to bluff your way through a major client document. That is neither professional nor acceptable. Is my message clear?"

"Yes, ma'am."

"Fortunately, for you, there were aspects of the report that were worthy to present to the client. Had that not been the case, this conversation would have been much shorter. I think you know what that means."

Casey knew he had dodged a bullet. He also knew he was tarnished in the eyes of his boss. "Yes, I do. It won't happen again."

"No, it won't."

Casey's eyes widened as he waited for Brandi to continue.

"You and I are going to meet every Wednesday morning at eight. You will brief me on your work and inform me of any problems or potential problems. You will also provide me a written status report by noon each Friday."

She paused to make sure he understood. "Casey, your past performance and your hard work earned you a second chance. I will view this as an anomaly, but it cannot happen again. We cannot have our reputation stained or lose multimillion dollar commissions."

Casey replied in a soft voice that reflected his relief. "Ms. Cobb, I know I messed up and appreciate you rescuing me. I never meant to put Mays and McCovey in a bad light with the client. What I did was unprofessional and inexcusable. No one is more grateful than I am that the deal wasn't lost. I just want to earn back your trust."

Brandi Cobb rose, walked over to her desk, retrieved a thick manila folder, and resumed her place at the table. "This," she began, "is a potential merger of two radio syndicates. Included are financial reports, preliminary FCC documents, meeting notes, and letters of intent. What I need from you is the market impact analysis and an estimate of the potential advertising revenue. It is due in six weeks, and I expect a final draft from you in three weeks.

"If you need any thing else, check with Gabriella."

"Thanks. I will complete it on time," said Casey, surprised by the assignment.

Casey left the meeting still oblivious to the trail of confused gators.

Brandi Cobb chooses the time-honored tradition of making people sweat before learning they are spared the axe. Instead of disciplining Casey Ruth by telephone, she lets him spend a sleepless night thinking about his mistake. Then she meets with him to discuss the problem and to make her expectations clear. Once she feels Casey understands, she offers him an opportunity to regain her trust.

To his credit, Casey listens and accepts the rebuke. He provides his boss an explanation, albeit late, instead of an excuse. He understands the consequences of his actions and his failure to act professionally and responsibly.

The gators are disappointed that their dinner wriggles off the hook. Or does he?

Ten days later, Casey again encountered an obstacle; he didn't have enough information to complete his analysis. He remembered Brandi's instructions to ask Gabriella for whatever he needed. He asked for help and received it.

Gabriella, Brandi's assistant, furnished him the names of two accounting managers who could supply the missing information. In two telephone calls he secured promises from each to send the information by overnight delivery.

Meeting with Brandi the next morning, he explained the status of the project. "There isn't enough data from the southeast and northeast markets to complete the advertising revenue projections."

Taking a deep breath, he continued, "This morning I called the accounting departments of both companies and asked them to send the data on CD-ROM by overnight carrier. I will have CDs tomorrow and can complete the draft earlier than scheduled."

Brandi skimmed the report, searching for key elements. She read paragraphs from several pages, then looked at Casey and smiled. "I think you have the situation under control. This draft is concise and addresses the major issues. Let me know if there is a delay with the advertising information. Very good work."

Casey was relieved. "Thank you."

Several gators, growing weak from starvation, slowly left the office, wondering if there was an accounting firm nearby.

Casey Ruth learns his lesson quickly and drives away the gators in his life.

Mistakes are part of growth, and growth comes from not repeating the same mistakes.

TWENTY-THREE

Don't Taunt the Gators

The final lesson.

You survive the crisis, achieve victory, and feel good about yourself. After a major victory, it is easy to forget that alligators are meaner and much faster than humans. They are also relentless in their desire to catch and devour prey. Speed, a relentless nature, and the desire for revenge are a dangerous combination in a reptile with sharp teeth.

If you see a gator basking in the sun or stretched out on the bank of a lake, don't taunt it. Gators are notorious for being poor losers; they bite anything that torments them. Instead of teasing them, walk by knowing that you just kicked some gator butt and will do so again if necessary.

Character, inner satisfaction, and quiet confidence are the results of success gained through perseverance.

If you foolishly tease a recently defeated gator, he or she may take offense and attack you. Which do you prefer, the quiet inner thrill of victory or the agony of surgery on the feet?

Sitting in his office, while reflecting on his escape from a group of gators, Zane Grove felt vindicated and invincible. As vice president of information technology for the management company, Robinson and Jackson, he was responsible for the company's recent computer conversion. A successful conversion, he might add. But that was only part of the story.

For reasons known only to him, Zane cut corners in the due diligence process. After that got into the rumor mill, he spent months denying that he benefited from the vendor selection. Robinson and Jackson employees speculated about what he may have received: cash, paid vacations, stock, or paid speaking engagements.

His aura of invincibility was pierced when he recalled the intense questioning from Simon Robinson. Simon, the managing partner, had attacked relentlessly and grilled him for over two hours. Zane was cool and prepared. He provided documentation to prove that he had investigated the vendors in compliance with corporate policy and selected the appropriate one. He also answered a number of questions about improper remuneration.

Zane is self-absorbed and oblivious to reality. He never considered that the mere implication of impropriety had damaged him in the eyes of his staff. He didn't realize that many members of the organization, including the partners, were not convinced he acted ethically. Nor did he comprehend Simon's careful wording, "There is no preponderance of evidence indicating improper remuneration." Not exactly an absolution.

Zane also missed three rather agitated and famished gators waiting in the shadows of his office.

Zane Grove is at a moral crossroad. He can continue to behave irresponsibly, or he can change and act responsibly.

Everyone arrives at this crossroad at least once in life, some more than once. Making the right choice isn't always easy, and the right choice isn't always self-evident. However, there are often signs warning you that your choice is incorrect. Unfortunately, the signs aren't always obvious or in plain sight. You have to look for them.

Zane has always tempted fate, choosing the daring route. Will he change?

Several weeks later, Simon Robinson scheduled a meeting with Zane to discuss the next major technology project: wireless connectivity between the company's three buildings. Instead of a vendor review, Robinson and Jackson would issue a "Request For Proposals" (RFP).

As he strutted down the hallway to Simon's office, Zane missed the gators silently crawling behind him.

Simon wanted to set a serious tone, so he measured his words carefully. "Zane, you need to understand that I would be remiss in my duties as managing partner not to review the wireless networking project in light of the questions raised from the recent conversion. I didn't require a written briefing last time and regret it. For this project, I want written reports on the first and fifteenth of each month. I also want you to meet with me each week for a verbal update. Is that clear and acceptable?"

"It is clear."

Simon chose not to comment and continued, saying, "We need to select a company that can perform the work with minimal interruption to our current network activity. I want limited downtime during normal business hours and want the project completed within six months."

When Zane didn't respond, he asked, "Do you think we should structure the proposal to require evening and weekend work to accomplish our goal of minimal work interruption?"

"Sure. Whatever you think."

Simon leaned forward. "Your petulance is unprofessional. I expect my CIO to conduct himself as a professional at all times. This project, having significant capital investment, is important. We cannot afford a considerable loss of access to our information. Your job is to minimize that risk. Am I clear?"

"Yes, sir."

"Can we structure the RFP for evening and weekend downtime without eliminating quality vendors?"

"Yes, it is common in some industries. Like healthcare and financial services."

"Good. What about the six month time frame? Is that a problem?"

Zane pretended to think before he spoke. "I think we can make it work. One or two potential candidates may drop out. Especially if they don't have the resources to commit right away."

"Is six months reasonable?"

Again Zane waited a few seconds. "I don't anticipate any problems that would extend it past six months. There are several aggressive companies that would die for the opportunity to win this contract."

"Do you have anyone in particular in mind?"

"No, that is just an observation."

Simon wasn't sure he believed Zane and hesitated. "Okay, I want you to prepare the RFP for my review by week's end. Have you thought about who would manage the project?"

"I want Trevor Durocher."

Simon tried to hide his surprise. "Zane, I am not comfortable with him running this project. He is a highly skilled technician, but he's very inexperienced, reactive, and has no project management experience."

Zane spoke defensively. "He was a big help to me during the conversion. He's earned it."

"Saving your butt from the frying pan does not qualify him to manage the project!" Simon barked. "I think you need to reconsider and give me an answer tomorrow morning."

Zane silently counted to three, then asked, "Would it raise your comfort level if you met with Trevor? I'm convinced he can do the job, and I think you will be too after you interview him. He is capable, energetic, eager, and, yes, he did work very hard on the conversion. Not to save me, but to ensure the project's success."

Simon stared at Zane. "Okay, I'll meet with him for fifteen minutes. I'm available at five-thirty today. But if I'm not one hundred percent convinced, do you agree to find someone else?"

Zane nodded slowly. "Yes."

After the meeting, Zane sat in his office, tossing wads at a bulls-eye on the wall.

> Either Trevor manages the project or Robinson and Jackson can complete the project without me, he thought. Simon can't afford to go through a major project without me and can't afford to delay this one while he finds a new CIO.
>
> Smugly congratulating himself for another coup, he missed hearing one of the gators using a cell phone to invite friends "to a party, really soon."

Zane is setting himself up for a fall, falsely thinking that he has Simon at a disadvantage. Zane doesn't know that Simon doesn't trust him and is discreetly searching for a replacement.

Thinking you will always outsmart the gators can lead you directly into their trap.

> Early the next morning Simon telephoned Zane, and he got right to the point, "Zane, I met with Trevor yesterday. I think he will be a fine project manager one day, but not yet."
>
> "What do you mean by that?"
>
> "Trevor doesn't have a strong grasp of the details, and I don't think he has enough savvy to work with management. There isn't any margin for error on this project."
>
> "I must say I am disappointed." Zane fumed and did not try to hide it.
>
> Simon, however, controlled his anger. "Disappointed or not, I want a list of candidates, internal and external, on my desk by noon today. We need to have the manager in place by the middle of next month so we can complete this project on time."
>
> "I'll see what I can do."
>
> "Zane, this isn't an option. For the project to be completed on time, we need a project manager in place. I want the list of candidates today—by noon. Please do as I request."
>
> "Request?" He continued boldly by saying, "You undermine my authority and have the nerve to call it a request? Maybe you'd like to try this project without me!" He was clearly becoming more irate.
>
> "Zane, you need to calm down and think about what you are saying. Nothing good can come from you challenging me.

It would be in your best interest to stop and think about the ramifications of your words. This is not the time for you to speak without thinking." Glancing at his watch, Simon added, "I will be free to meet with you in forty-five minutes. We can revisit this issue at that time."

"I'll be there," Zane said, before hanging up.

The gators began salivating and mentally dividing Zane into sections; each gator knew that the real treat was Zane's oversized ego.

Zane walks right into a trap, blinded by ego and pride. He believes he is invincible and irreplaceable. He not only doesn't see the gators, he doesn't see the swamp, either.

Seconds after he cradled the phone, Simon Robinson located a folder containing the resumes of interim CIO candidates and placed it in his briefcase. He thought that he might need to contact a few of them this evening.

Next Simon called the network administrator, spoke briefly, and asked her to stand by for another call within ninety minutes.

Zane was busy typing two documents. One was his resignation, the other was his wish list. He envisioned using the wish list as a bargaining chip after Simon begged him to rescind his resignation and remain with Robinson and Jackson.

Zane carried a portfolio containing the two documents as he marched toward Simon's office. Several very merry gators followed him. They had sipped Merlot while he typed his resignation, and now they were ready to party.

Entering Simon's reception area, Zane opened the door to the inner office without knocking or waiting for an invitation. Simon was reading a document and acknowledged him with a wave. "Do you mind if I finish this?"

Zane walked to the side table and pulled out a chair. "Take your time." Zane's cockiness was apparent.

Simon finished reading and joined Zane at the table. With the skill of a seasoned executive, he began by saying, "We're both reasonable men, maybe a bit headstrong at times. Do you think we can resolve this?"

"Simon, I think we need to clear the air first."

"Okay. Go ahead."

Zane leaned forward and rested his elbows on his knees. Making steeples with his fingers, he said, "I feel very strongly that Trevor should manage this project. As CIO, I have an inherent right to choose the project manager, and I don't appreciate you overruling me. It undermines my credibility with my staff."

"I see. What else?"

"Selecting someone else internally will take time. If we hire outside the company, there isn't time for them to learn our systems and infrastructure. Either way will jeopardize our six month deadline."

Simon stared at the table, then looked up. He spoke in a firm voice. "Zane, are you willing to compromise? Trevor can be the number two guy, but not the project manager."

Zane smirked. "Either Trevor is the project manager or I resign."

Simon shook his head and smiled. "Okay."

His ego running rampant, Zane snorted. "I knew you would see it my way."

"No, you don't understand. I accept your resignation."

Zane's jaw dropped and his eyes narrowed. "You must be crazy! How do you plan to complete this project without me as the CIO?"

Simon picked up his phone and dialed the network administrator. When she answered, he spoke calmly. "This is Simon Robinson, please deactivate Mr. Grove's access to all systems and functions immediately. I'll determine the reallocation of his duties within the next twenty-four hours. Thank you."

He replaced the phone and looked at Zane "You will be escorted from the building by two security officers. You can call human resources tomorrow and make arrangements to retrieve your personal belongings.

> "Do not attempt to re-enter the building or access any computer files. I will arrange for someone to call you and download any personal files onto CDs for you."
>
> He rose and ushered a stunned Zane to the door. The security guards, who had been waiting in the hallway, met them. "Good luck, Zane. You did some very good work here. I'm sorry it had to end like this." He offered his hand to the departing CIO.
>
> Zane sneered and walked out.
>
> One of the security guards turned to the other and said, "Is it my imagination or do I hear 'Crocodile Rock'?"
>
> "Man, I thought it was just me."
>
> As Zane continued to walk down the hall, the gators closed the gap, prepared to enjoy a hearty meal and a victory party.

Zane dances on the edge of the cliff one time too many. As result, he falls into the waiting mouths of hungry gators.

No one can expect to win every gamble. Professional gamblers are happy if they win a little over half of the time. Zane Grove thinks he is the exception and will win every toss of the dice; instead, he becomes the victim of his ego and reckless abandon.

This round goes to the gators, who don't even have to work for their meal. Their victim's ego did the work for them.

TWENTY-FOUR

The Lessons

In each scenario, from Nick Koufax's realization in "Remember The Original Mission" to Zane Grove's ego-driven fall in "Don't Taunt the Gators," we observe how people deal with the gators in their lives. Each chapter contains at least one lesson that you can apply when you are in a gator-filled swamp. Here are all thirty-two lessons; consider them a primer for fighting gators.

1. Don't tick off the gators.
2. Remember the original mission.
3. Focus on the mission, not the problems and fears.
4. The goal is to get away from the gators, not to further antagonize them.
5. Change your plan to fit the circumstances.
6. Focus on the hungriest gators first.
7. All problems are not created equal—some are subsets. Solve the primary ones before attempting to defeat their progeny.

8. Deal with reality; don't waste energy or time fighting make-believe foes.
9. Find a solution, not just an escape.
10. Ask for and accept help. It is a sign of applied intelligence, not weakness.
11. Use the shovel wisely; dig out, not deeper.
12. Never sacrifice another human being to advance your career or cause.
13. You may only get one chance to distract the gators; use it to your advantage.
14. Use your mind and the available resources to escape the gators, just as McGyver would do.
15. Don't waste bullets; aim your shots wisely.
16. Outwit them or outwait them.
17. When enemies surround you, be your own best friend.
18. To control a situation, you must first control yourself.
19. Stand up to the bully.
20. Trust your instincts.
21. Take control of your life and get rid of the gators.
22. To complete the mission you must solve the problem(s) that placed you in the swamp.
23. Be man or woman enough to shoulder the blame if you caused the problem. If someone else is at fault, be gracious and merciful, as you may need mercy and grace one day.
24. Expect an occasional gator assault.
25. Every good plan includes escape routes.
26. The meek may inherit the earth, but the resilient will accomplish much more prior to the end of the world.
27. Mistakes are part of growth and growth comes from not repeating the same mistakes.

28. After a major victory, it is easy to forget that alligators are meaner and much faster than humans. They are also relentless in their desire to catch and devour prey.
29. Making the right choice isn't always easy or self-evident; however, there are often signs to warn you that your choice is incorrect. Unfortunately, the signs aren't always obvious or in plain sight. You have to look for them.
30. To think you will always outsmart the gators can lead you directly into their trap. Blinded by ego and pride, you will walk directly into the gator's trap.
31. Pushing your luck too many times results in a victory party for the gators.
32. Don't taunt the gators!

Suggested Reading

Like many writers, I enjoy reading, and I spend an inordinate amount of time in libraries and bookstores. Books open your mind to new ideas and help you find answers. Many books contain keys to managing your life and problems. The following are among my favorites, and most are available in a variety of formats, including hardcover, softcover, mass market paperback and audio book.

The Art of Exceptional Living by Jim Rohn. Motivational ideas for daily success.

Feel the Fear and Do It Anyway: Dynamic Techniques for Turning Fear, Indecision, and Anger Into Power, Action, and Love by Susan Jeffers, Ph.D. The boost you need to overcome fear of failure.

How to Win Friends & Influence People by Dale Carnegie. This remains the Bible of relationships in business and life.

InVINCEable Principles: Essential Tools for Life Mastery! by Vince Poscente. An excellent book about life mastery.

The Leadership Secrets of Colin Powell by Oren Harari. Practical leadership ideas from one of America's greatest leaders.

Man's Search For Meaning by Viktor Frankl. A concentration camp survivor's advice on the importance of attitude in our lives.

Principle-Centered Leadership by Stephen R. Covey. A handbook for keeping integrity in your personal and professional life.

Reinventing Yourself: How to Become the Person You've Always Wanted to Be by Steve Chandler. Eye-opening—are you an owner or a victim?

See You at the Top by Zig Ziglar (a revised edition of *Biscuits, Fleas, and Pump Handles*). A reminder of the need for integrity in our lives.

Zapp! The Lightning of Empowerment: How to Improve Productivity, Quality, and Employee Satisfaction by William C. Byham, Ph.D., with Jeff Cox. Empowerment ideas you can put into practice immediately and see results.

Index

A

"Accept help", 39, 41, 137, 156
"Aim your shots wisely", 69, 156
analysis, 14–15, 18, 22, 24, 131, 144
  of the situation, 12, 37, 72, 97
"Analyze the situation", 12, 37, 72, 97
"Apply what you learn", 12, 41, 61, 63–64, 136–37, 156
"Assess the situation", 12, 63, 77, 110

B

bullets, 65, 69, 156
  dodging, 143
bullies, 90, 95, 98, 105, 156 (*see also* "Stand up to the bully")
Byham, William C., 160

C

Carnegie, Dale, 136, 159
Chandler, Steve, 160
character, 29, 55–56, 66, 131, 147
"Complete the project", 22, 27–28, 31, 114, 117, 151, 163
confidence, 15, 26, 50, 61–63, 67, 73, 85, 88–89, 91–92, 94, 97, 99, 100–101, 103, 115–16, 121, 140, 147
control, 11, 13, 35, 57, 59–60, 82, 85, 109, 113, 127–30, 139, 145, 151, 164
  of yourself, 83, 156
Covey, Steven R., 160
Cox, Jeff, 160

INDEX

crossroad
   moral, 148
   personal, 128, 148, 162

D

"Deal with reality", 30, 156 (*see also* reality)
"Develop a plan", 35, 43–44, 55, 83, 163 (*see also* plans)
"Distract the gators", 54–55, 71, 83, 109, 125, 156, 163
distraction, 54, 71, 83, 109
"Don't waste bullets", 65, 156 (*see also* bullets)
"Don't taunt the gators", 147, 155, 157
"Don't aggravate the gators", 43, 99, 127, 130

E

egos, 73, 79, 126, 130, 152–55, 157
emotions, 83, 126, 139, 162
   removal of, 72
   separation of, 74
escapes, 12, 35, 37, 41, 43, 45, 47, 55, 61, 62, 64, 69, 88, 97, 119, 124–26, 131, 139–40, 147, 156
examples, 62, 68, 89, 113, 115, 142

F

fears, 11, 22, 31, 64, 71, 74, 83–86, 89, 129, 140, 155, 159
   facing your, 85, 88, 163
   of failure, 17
   overcoming your, 75
first priority, 17, 163

flexibility, 107, 110, 113, 119, 124, 139–40
focus, 12–13, 17–19, 27, 30–31, 37, 41, 43–45, 47, 51, 55–56, 74, 88, 115, 134, 155
Frankl, Viktor, 160
frustration, 16, 40

G

growth, 135, 145, 156

H

Harari, Oren, 160
help, 12–13, 25–27, 34, 36–37, 39–41, 45, 48, 50, 62, 64, 69, 71, 78–81, 89–90, 97, 101–104, 107, –110, 113–15, 119, 125–26, 134, 136–37, 139, 141–44, 150, 156, 159, 163
honesty, 24, 29, 54, 77, 97, 131
hungriest gator, the, 27, 31, 155
hungry gator, a, 98, 129, 154

I

identification, 28, 34, 37, 72, 74, 78, 82, 132,
instincts, 107, 156
integrity, 29, 31, 53, 160

J

Jeffers, Susan, 159

K

knowledge, 16, 61, 86, 132, 152, 162
   application of, 12, 41, 61, 63–64, 136–37, 156

L

"Lead and protect", 119

"Lead by example", 89

leaders, 65, 72, 89, 98, 140 (*see also* leading)

leadership, 18, 33, 63, 71, 82, 89, 110, 119, 151, 157 (*see also* leaders)

learning, 12, 13, 34–35, 41, 57–58, 69, 77, 79, 83, 90, 98, 102, 110, 129, 131, 136–37, 144–45, 153 (*see also* knowledge)

lessons, 12–13, 99, 145, 147, 155

life, 12–14, 36, 51, 54, 65, 82, 92, 98, 107, 128, 130–31, 139, 145, 148, 156, 159, 160–62

M

McGyver, Angus, 61–62, 64, 124, 156

missions, 11, 14, 18, 21, 23, 38, 45, 47, 50–51, 60, 83, 125, 131, 139, 142–43, 156

original, 13, 17, 19, 24, 155

mistakes, 14, 40, 48, 50, 51, 77, 79, 120, 134, 144–45, 156

"Mistakes are part of growth", 145, 156

modifications, 28, 104, 113, 121

"Modify your plan", 104, 113 (*see also* plans)

morality, 53, 148, 162 (*see also* moral crossroad)

moral crossroad, 148 (*see also* crossroad)

O

original mission, 13, 17, 19, 24, 155 (*see also* missions)

overcoming, 13, 19, 75, 84, 159

P

personal crossroad, 128, 148, 162

plans, 12, 18, 21, 23–24, 26, 33, 38, 58, 62–63, 66, 74, 79, 86, 90, 92, 94–95, 97–103, 107–109, 115, 117, 119, 121, 124, 126, 133–34, 139, 153, 155–56, 64

development of, 35, 43–44, 55, 83, 163

modification of, 104, 113

S*ee also* moral crossroad

plunging, 88, 163

Poscente, Vince, 159

presentations, 15, 18, 22, 62–64, 67, 72, 100, 102, 119–23, 164

priorities, 15, 17, 37, 78, 81, 163

problems, 11–15, 22, 24, 29–31, 36, 41, 43–45, 47, 53–57, 59, 61–62, 64, 66, 68–69, 71–72, 77–81, 83, 85, 89–90, 94, 97–98, 107, 109, 117, 122, 127–28, 131–32, 135–37, 140–41, 143–44, 149–50, 155–56, 159, 163

focus on, 115

identifying the, 37, 74, 82

the real, 17, 37, 74

projects, 14–16, 18–19, 22–23, 25–28, 31, 33, 37, 40–41, 45, 48, 50, 54–55, 73, 89–91, 102, 108, 114, 116–17, 121, 145, 149–51, 153, 163

protection, 64, 119

R

reality, 30, 77, 97–98, 104, 141, 148, 156, 163
reclaimed control of his life, 130
reclamation, 128
    control of life, 130
removal, 15, 26, 29, 72, 82, 93, 119, 162
"Remove the emotion", 72
responsibilities, 29, 88, 144, 148
Rohn, Jim, 159

S

self-control, 82 (*see also* control)
separation, 12, 22
    of emotions, 74
shots, 22–23, 65, 69, 79, 101, 105, 156
shovels, 13, 47, 51, 156, 164
situations, 11, 13, 17, 21, 35–36, 43, 62–63, 71, 74, 83–84, 90, 94, 98, 104, 107, 110, 113, 126, 129, 131, 141, 145, 156
    analysis of, 12, 37, 72, 97
solutions, 12, 14, 22–24, 37, 43, 53, 60–64, 69, 77, 79, 81, 97, 109, 148, 156
    alternate, 60
    focusing on the, 115
    presenting the, 22
"Solve the problem", 11–12, 17, 29–31, 37, 43–45, 47, 56–57, 61–62, 64–65, 69, 71–72, 74, 78, 81–83, 85, 89, 97, 107, 109, 117, 128, 131, 137, 140, 153, 155–156

"Stand up to the bully", 90, 156 (*see also* bullies)
stress, 90
swamps, 12,–14, 17, 28, 35, 39–40, 43, 45, 47, 75, 77, 97–98, 104, 119, 121, 124–25, 131–32, 139–40, 152, 155–56

T

"Take control", 13, 113, 156
    of your life, 128
"Think first", 62
time, 12, 15–16, 18, 21–23, 27–29, 33, 35–37, 39, 41, 44–45, 47, 53, 58, 60–61, 63, 66–69, 71–72, 77–79, 81, 83–87, 89–93, 97–98, 100, 103–104, 107–108, 113, 115–16, 119–21, 123–26, 129–30, 132, 134, 137, 140, 143–44, 149, 151–54, 156–57, 159
    wasting, 17, 30–31, 50–51, 65, 141, 142
trust, 62, 85, 87, 109, 117, 144, 151, 156, 164
    of your instincts, 107
truth, 11, 13, 49, 53, 56, 73, 92, 94, 110, 113
    facing the, 133

U

"Use the shovel wisely", 47 (*see also* shovels; wisdom)

W

waste, 18, 45, 48, 81, 83, 120
    of bullets, 65, 156
    of time, 17, 30–31, 50–51, 65, 141, 142
weapons, 65, 69, 115
wisdom, 16, 30, 47, 65, 69, 141, 156–64

Z

Ziglar, Zig, 160

About the Author

Jim Grigsby faced problems similar to events depicted in this book; some are the basis for case studies. Throughout his career he worked with trying people; he worked for extremely demanding, micro-managing, and, in some cases, unethical bosses; and he managed 51 employees in a multi-departmental environment. Experience taught him the importance of identifying the core issue and working to solve the problem.

Jim escaped gator-filled swamps many times! While surrounded by gators, he maintained his sense of humor, learned valuable lessons, and preserved his sanity. Success and failure taught him the thirty-two lessons portrayed in this book. He is willing to share those lessons through his writings and presentations.

An Economics and Mathematics major at Western Michigan University, Jim is now the Director of Client Development for a national healthcare consulting firm. He previously held various management positions in healthcare and consumer finance.

Jim Grigsby is an active member of the Florida chapter of the Healthcare Financial Management Association (HFMA) and a former national officer in the American Association of Healthcare Management (AAHAM).

As a Certified Patient Accounts Manager and Certified Document Imaging Architech, Jim has authored dozens of articles in the healthcare realm, including the AAHAM's 1991 National Editor's Award winning, "Financial Counseling And The Chemical Dependency Patient". He is a highly sought national speaker on healthcare revenue cycle management, healthcare technology, professional certification, and business process disaster recovery programs.

If you wish to schedule Jim Grigsby for a presentation of *Don't Tick Off The Gators! Managing Problems Before Problems Manage You* or an interview, please contact him at JimGrigsbyBooks.com.

Jim and his family live on Florida's Treasure Coast, where he is writing his second book: *Are You Surrounded By Jerks?*—an irreverent guide to dealing with the annoying people who surround you at work, at play and in your personal life.

Don't Tick Off The Gators! **Presentations**

Jim Grigsby wants to help you escape the gators in your life and is available for *Don't Tick Off The Gators! Managing Problems Before Problems Manage You* presentations to groups and businesses.

A 90-minute presentation customized for your group will provide an engaging, humorous slant on the scenarios and lessons in *Don't Tick Off The Gators! Managing Problems Before Problems Manage You.* Attendees will learn how to apply the book's lessons in their business or personal life.

Jim has enjoyed public speaking since he was 14 years old and participated in the Optimists International Speech Contest. Although he didn't win the contest, he developed a love for speaking that continues to be a large part of his professional life today.

Don't Tick Off The Gators! Managing Problems Before Problems Manage You is for anyone who faces gators every day:

- Business and Professional Associations
- Educational and Coaching Associations
- Business Conventions
- Employers—large, medium, and small
- Schools—from Junior High through MBA programs
- Youth Groups
- Church Groups
- Civic Organizations
- Libraries

Please visit www.JimGrigsbyBooks.com to learn more about *Don't Tick Off The Gators! Managing Problems Before Problems Manage You* presentations and how you can qualify for a bulk discount on books for your attendees. You may also inquire directly by sending an email to: presentations@JimGrigsbyBooks.com.